Philosophy and Its Shadow

European Perspectives
A Series of the Columbia University Press

Philosophy and Its Shadow

Eugenio Trías

Translated by Kenneth Krabbenhoft

COLUMBIA UNIVERSITY PRESS
New York
1983

Library of Congress Cataloging in Publication Data

Trías, Eugenio, 1942–
Philosophy and its shadow.

(European perspectives)
Translation of: La filosofía y su sombra.
Includes bibliographical references and index.
1. Philosophy. I. Title. II. Series.
B53.T7313 1982 100 82-12803
ISBN 0-231-05288-X

Spanish edition: *La Filosofía y su Sombra*
Copyright © 1969 Eugenio Trías

Columbia University Press
New York   Guildford, Surrey

*Clothbound editions of Columbia Press books are Smyth-sewn and printed
on permanent and durable acid-free paper.*

Contents

Philosophy and Its Shadow

1
Philosophy and Its Shadow

FOR a number of decades metaphysics inspired profound scorn and self-righteous terror among scientists and philosophers. The metaphysician was thought to bed down indiscriminately with shady creatures like Being and Nothingness, and from their unwholesome union was said to issue a brood of verbal monsters endowed with undeniable magic powers but totally lacking in meaning. How could anyone speak without shame of "spirit," "consciousness," "matter," "praxis," or "Being"? It was time to curb these expressions or purge them altogether from our language. They had to be explicitly forbidden or tabooed to prevent their use.

This "fear of metaphysics" also meant that the rules which sanctioned or condemned verbal promiscuity and the abuse of certain ambiguities common to "everyday speech" had to be specified. These rules against traveling certain roads or uttering certain words resemble nothing more than the incest taboo operative in the realm of sexuality. This sexual nuance remains at the very core of metaphysics, where "healthy" consciousness looks down on "intimacy with Being." For the scientist to dabble with metaphysics meant, in other words, that he was guilty of incest.

The only "healthy" or "civilized" stance to take in the matter of scientific well-being was consequently to denounce and "expose" the scandal. So-called "logical analysis," "methodology," and sociology joined hands to this end. The former's task was to reveal the logical errors and syntactical defects of metaphysical discourse, while "methodology" identified the "non-contrastability" of its statements and sociology pointed out the evolution, scope, and place of the "mythical" content of metaphysical discourse.

Today these often repeated condemnations are becoming tiresome. We have heard all too often that metaphysics is meaningless because it breaks the rules for forming meaningful statements, because it lacks an "empirical basis," because it employs polyvalent terms and so forth ad nauseam. More seriously, however, this persistent singsong has kept us from knowing the thing we are condemning. We have not been able to discover if we are condemning something that really exists or merely conjuring evil spirits. Some present-day logicians still wage war against imaginary giants (when there are only dwarfs left to fight) in a second-rate cartoon version of the heroic pathos of logical positivism in the 1930s. This "witch hunt" has an obsessive character, and in the end it widens the scope of denunciation to unexpected dimensions. This insipid "logicalism," like all forms of narrow rationalism, eventually leads to the worst kind of irrationalism, the kind that makes no effort to understand, rejecting what it does not already know.

1. From Anathema to Dialogue

This mentality of denunciation and "exposé" seems both sterile and sterilizing today, as it makes it difficult for us fully to comprehend, explain and *know* what metaphysical discourse *is*. It is not enough to say that Heidegger fails to take logical syntax into account or that he invents nonsensical phrases like "nothing swims in nothingness." What we need to know and understand is the "inner logic" of Heidegger's discourse. We need to analyze its structure and isolate the internal laws which determine how statements are generated within it. Logical analysis as wielded by logical positivism and simplistic analytical philosophy is extrinsic analysis: it does not help us to understand the object under analysis.

Likewise, to seek an explanation of metaphysical discourse on an entirely different level, such as sociology or societal politics, is fruitless. The sociological approach to knowledge believes that all discourse expresses given social contents. This is quite true, but it also believes that these contents are the "true contents" of discourse. In other words, the sociological approach transforms the social content into the "overall content" of texts. Lukács' mistake in *The Young Hegel* and *The Destruction of Reason* was to accept without questioning these methodological assumptions which require that the interpreter distort the text in order to make it "express" meanings which become apparent solely as functions of the interpreter's patience and hypnotic power. Now, this approach obviously rejects an immanent analysis of the text out of hand, at times denying the feasibility of such an analysis in the name of nineteenth-century social determinism. Finally, this kind of approach attempts to relate a set of already known phenomena, like "economic structures," to an as yet unknown set of phenomena like the still-undiscovered "structure of metaphysical discourse." A known structure, in other words, is brought into relation with random elements of an unknown structure.

But the primary obstacle to our analyzing and understanding metaphysical discourse resides in neither the extrinsic nature of logical analysis nor in the methodological weakness of the sociological approach to knowledge and related "ideological criticism." It lies rather in the tacit or explicit contention that such discourse is "nonsensical" and "irrational." If it did not raise our suspicions, this contention would stop us from inquiring into the "inherent rationalism" of metaphysical discourse.

What do we understand by "nonsense" and "irrationality"? I honestly believe that there is no answer to this question, which strikes me as what the "Neopositivists" themselves mean by a "poorly stated question." We can nevertheless understand the mental code of those individuals who are fond of distinguishing between meaningful and meaningless human activities and discourse. In their "clarity" we detect a vice inherited from their ancestors the

Manicheans, who were so adept at differentiating Right and Wrong. The Manicheans bequeathed the notion to the history of mankind, and we have received it directly from the Enlightenment.

The modern social sciences have taken upon themselves precisely the task of clearing away this mirage. They have discovered coherence and rationality in the speech of the so-called "insane" as well as in the social institutions and myths of the so-called "primitive" societies. The domains of religion and mythology, traditionally held to be the most resistant to rational analysis, have in the end delivered up their "inherent logic." A "theo-logic" that presided over the Indo-European pantheon has been unearthed as well as a "mytho-logic" underlying the myths of the New World.[1]

Given this state of affairs, will we continue to deny the rational nature of those magnificent myths of our culture that for convenience's sake we call "metaphysical systems"? Would it not be more prudent to avoid hasty judgments and dedicate ourselves to a deep analysis of those systems, to substitute analysis for condemnation and dialogue for anathema?

Will it not also be possible to exchange the tools of condemnation for implements of a finer variety? Will we not in this sense be able to equip ourselves with the analytical tools that have enabled science to conquer the realms of religion and myth, until now so resistant to structuring?

2. Methodology

If we were to answer these questions we would approach a number of texts with different methodologies and afterward weigh and evaluate the results. This task goes beyond our immediate objectives, however, which are simply to propose a few summary objections to the traditional "academic" methods and indicate a possible alternative.

The most successful approaches in the area of metaphysics (and, in general, the "history of philosophy") have by and large gone to three different extremes. The empirical extreme has led to mere chronological dating, "glosses" and "commentaries" of texts. The historicist extreme has sanctified the notions of "influence," "synthesis," "evolution," and "development" as the basic categories of analysis. The classifying extreme has slapped a specific label on the forehead of each type of discourse ("idealist," "rationalist," "materialist," etc.).

In practice these three extremes have acted in unison. They have long been the only "sane" alternative to the normative kind of philosophical history. Empiricism basically prevented us from ridding ourselves of those "reconstructions" of the history of philosophy formally inspired by Hegel. These always presupposed a certain philosophy of history and a definite belief in the system (Kantian, in Cassirer's case; Thomist, in Maréchal's).[2] Light was shed on the past and future of philosophies—the former usually understood as "seed" and the latter as "decay"—by appeal to a definite system, which was assumed to state the most important philosophical problems correctly. Empiricism performed the laudable task of critically establishing, glossing, and commenting on the representative texts of these polemical histories of philosophy and cautiously describing the relationships between the systems. To this end it tended to make use of the philosophers' own categories and definitions. As a consequence empiricism usually classified their systems by pairing them in opposing "genera": rationalism/empiricism, idealism/realism, spiritualism/materialism, immanentism/transcendentalism, monism/pluralism, substantivism/phenomenalism, etc.

Because of the combination of empiricism and the urge to categorize, both the general histories and the monographs of a specific period remained at the level of mere description. When they unfortunately ventured beyond that level they arrived at conclusions they could not substantiate: as if by way of compensation, they added vacuous "explanations," based on arbitrary classifications, to the existing descriptions. The arbitrary aspect was due to an apparently irresoluble difficulty: either one took advantage, in the heat of empiricist zeal, of classifications forged in the furnace of existing analyses of philosophy (one spoke consequently of Feuerbach's "materialism") or one used a criterion which was "extrinsic" to the work in question. In the first instance, any and all statements made by a philosopher about his or another thinker's works were considered valid. One was guilty of gullibility, of mistaking the discourse itself for its agent's consciousness of it. Consequently, one did not get beyond the "conscious level," as Marx would say, of "what men think about themselves," and unlike Marx one did not understand that what one says often does not coincide with what one *does*. In the second instance, quite to the contrary, classifications "consecrated" by use were assumed to be valid, and no one questioned whether they were appropriate for understanding the work in question.

There is no apparent solution to this problem: we cannot free ourselves of naive gullibility or arbitrary conformity. Taking into account the distance in time, this mixture of empiricism and classifying zeal offers certain analogies to the state of ethnology before the methodological revolution created by Lévi-Strauss.[3] The history of philosophy has also turned out to be a "butterfly collection" organized along the axes of system and chronology. Although each member of the collection bears a date and a label indicating his genus (idealist, materialist, etc.), no one has taken the time to question the legitimacy of these categories.

We believe nevertheless that this dilemma can be eradicated by use of a method which goes beyond both descriptive empiricism and the classifying urge, a method which retains the positive aspects of both while overcoming their respective weaknesses.

Ideally, this method obeys the empiricist principle of beginning with a clear description of the object of study. At the same time it rejects the notion that simple observation and description can justify generalizations or comparative explanations.

By the same token, this method emulates the principle underlying all classifications, that is, the necessity of creating a conceptual plan or "model" for organizing the material at hand. At the same time, it avoids the arbitrariness of categories.

Once the text or group of texts has been described, this method therefore attempts to select or isolate a number of aspects that can be seen in their actual or possible relationships. This step may be called "abstraction."[4] This "abstraction" is not the goal of the investigation, however, but rather its opposite: it is its true *starting point*. Once a certain number of relationships have been established, the method attempts to build a model which connects, so to speak, various sets of relationships.

At that point the material which has been described should be discarded. Working with the model alone, the series of operations made possible by the combined relationships should then be carried out. In this way other materials that might fit in the model may be established a priori and their general configuration predicted beforehand.

Although Leach serves as a kind of distant inspiration and stimulus, we have absolutely no intention of emulating his magnificent proof of the value of models in the field of ethnology. Using pure concepts based on mathematics, Leach demonstrates that societies may exist in which neither maternity nor paternity are recognized in the accepted sociological sense. He then substantiates the conclusions he draws from his model with ethnographical data.[5] But while ethnology is now in full bloom, the history of philosophy is still trapped in the vicious circle of scientific backwardness characterized by the problem we have been discussing. Under these conditions it is impossible to avoid a certain amount of mimicry and a certain poverty in our conclusions. What matters is to break the circle at some point, even if we must often fail at the outset.

We will therefore restrict ourselves to building a "suitable model." Its only goal is to suggest a stimulating path of investigation: there is therefore no question of it being a "true model."[6]

Let us recall for a moment the well-known chapter of *Nausea* in which Roquentin, the protagonist, is describing a tree he is looking at. Following *Being and Nothingness*, we can define Roquentin as a "subjectivity," a man who, because he is a man, is "condemned to be free" and finds himself in a world of solid, lifeless things which, we might say, exist fully "in themselves." These things (paper, table, tree, hand) are what they are for all eternity. Eternal and "necessary," they are the center of resistance to that hole or "nothingness of being" which is free human subjectivity.

At the same time, Roquentin has been given the responsibility of revealing the *meaning* of that solid object in front of him. He goes up to the tree, he describes it, he uncovers its meanings. He, Roquentin, an individual human being, is the condition or *ground* of the meanings of all things.

This is the general description. Let us now isolate some of the elements of the first paragraph:

1. Realm of freedom: Individual (Roquentin)
   Realm of necessity: Natural Object (tree)

From now on we can do without the description and even the terms in parentheses, focusing our attention on the two terms, which correspond to different axes: the Individual and the Natural Object. Let us try to erect a makeshift model which relates each of these terms to others that we can assume to be *in opposition*. In each case we will have to examine the relevance or irrelevance of the suggested opposition.

2. a) Realm of freedom: Individual/Group
   b) Realm of necessity: Natural Object/Cultural Object

Are these opposing terms relevant? Do they make up the *paradigm* on which Sartre based his choice of one or the other member of each pair of opposites? We must commute the terms of each pair of opposites in order to find the answer.

The result is as follows: If we substitute a *human group* for Roquentin we undercut *Nausea,* because the group, as a group, does not belong to the realm of freedom, which is the sole unalienable domain of individual subjectivity. In any event the group as such divides into a multiplicity of freedoms. The pair of opposites is therefore relevant.

The proof of its relevance is to be found elsewhere, in another Sartrean extreme *where the opposite term of the paradigm becomes apparent,* that is, in the *Critique of Dialectical Reason.* In this work the *revolutionary group* is defined by its *freedom* in contrast to the "necessity" that characterizes what is "practical and inert." This text shows therefore that the other, *invisible* term latent in the syntagmatic chain but *inhibited,* so to speak, in the earlier work, takes the place of the term which is *evident* in that work. The roles are switched only in Sartre's mature work.

The pair of opposites (a) is therefore *relevant. The system of options is what underlies Sartre's choices in the syntagmatic realm.* In a broader sense this analysis helps us to be on our guard against fruitless debates on the "evolution" or "non-evolution" of the so-called "second Sartre." We can state in this regard that there is no *break* between the two, because both the first and the second Sartre when viewed in this way can be seen to rely on the same *system.* The first and the second Sartre are neither more nor less than the two choices which can be made in a system which allows two options.

If on the other hand we try to alter the syntagmatic chain of *Nausea* by substituting the opposite corresponding term of pair (b), we find that the chain does not change. In effect, if we substitute a cultural artifact like a chair, an inkwell, or an automobile for the natural object "tree," we realize that all of these objects will arouse similar feelings in Roquentin. This is proven by the presence throughout the novel of objects with the same characteristics. The reason for this is clear: whatever the object, it is still a "thing" which exists "in-itself." . . . Consequently the opposition is not relevant but rather *redundant.* The same holds true for the *Critique of Dialectical Reason,* where "inert" things are as much "natural things," so to speak, as they are "reified social structures." Consequently,

a) Individual/Group
b) Natural Object = Sociocultural Artifact

Let us now take a look at the second paragraph of our description. We showed that for Sartre the individual human subjectivity is the *ground* for the meanings of all things, whether natural or socio-cultural. By themselves these things have no meaning: they *receive* meaning only by virtue of the subject's activity in revealing their meaning. They are *not*, therefore, the ground of meaning. In order to clarify their relationship to the ground of meaning we will say, for lack of a better expression, that they belong to the realm of *grounded things*. In the work of Sartre's maturity the ground of meaning is comprised by the revolutionary group, and to this group is assigned a *hermeneutical function*, as in Lukács' *History and Class Consciousness*. The totality of *grounded things* in Sartre's mature work, however, has not changed in relation to the early works.

3. c) Ground: Individual/Group
   d) Grounded Things: Nature = Culture

Despite our complete failure to understand relationship (d) in terms of an opposition, *let us suppose that such an opposition exists,* even at the risk of repeating our categories, and combine (c) and (d). The result is as follows:

	A	B	C	D
4. Ground:	Individual	Group	Individual	Group
Grounded Things:	Nature	Nature	Culture	Culture

Figures C and D are redundant with respect to A and B, respectively, since the terms can be *switched* without causing any significant alteration in the syntagmatic chain.

But let us now consider the relationship of (c) and (d) to a third term, (e), which corresponds to the pair of oppositions *ground/grounded things*. The relevance of this pair is obvious from the point of view of both *Being and Nothingness* and the *Critique of Dialectical Reason*. In both cases, however, it takes the form of diagram 4: it never results in any of the possible combinations which correspond to the inversion of the preceding model. These are as follows:

	A'	B'	C'	D'
4'. Ground:	Nature	Nature	Culture	Culture
Grounded Things:	Individual	Group	Individual	Group

When we relate (e) to (c) and (d) we realize that it is not enough to take into account Sartre's early texts. If we want to retrieve the system underlying these relationships we must examine other texts which correspond to the pattern of diagram 4', the continuation of diagram 4.

We will propose the following hypothesis on the basis of the complete model (4-4'): while the various terms corresponding to the "ground axis" are always in a relationship of opposition and are therefore relevant, the relationships corresponding to the "grounded axis" are all equivalent, redundant, and easily substituted. To prove this we will examine B' and D', keeping in mind that they are inversions of diagrams B and D along axis (e). Let us remember that we have agreed to consider B and D interchangeable.

For this purpose we will consider a few aspects of Freud and Lévi-Strauss which may fit the diagrams generated by our model.

Any philosophy of type B' should hold that the ground of sense and meaning of *social* acts is to be found in a *natural* component. No doubt quite a few philosophies considered "naturalistic" fall into this category, above all those which *derive* the meaning of acts and behavior from *natural* phenomena like drives and instincts. Freudianism, which explains the meaning of social institutions (the rules of kinship, religion, art, morality) in terms of conflicting instincts and drives, fits perfectly into this category. Now, this statement of the facts does not allow "culture" to substitute for "nature" (quite the contrary: "cultural artifacts" also derive their meaning from instinct). A philosophy of type D', on the other hand, would derive the meaning of acts, behavior, and social institutions from "cultural structures" of an "objective" sort. We therefore arrive at Lévi-Strauss, for whom the sense and meaning of all social acts and institutions is found in that "thing" or "object" which constitutes the "unconscious spirit of culture" and which can be distinguished, if only methodologically, from "nature." The key to the meaning of social institutions is found, in effect, not in nature but in the universal structures of culture. The incest taboo, for instance, is nothing more than the incursion of culture into nature. It founds a "new order" characterized by autonomy, rationality, and a special importance. Therefore:

$$B = D \mathbin{/\!/} 4': B'/D'$$

In diagram 4', however, A' and B' are redundant, as are C' and D'. The Freudian tenet that *social* behavior grows out of natural phenomena is confused with the notion that individual behavior is an instance of ontogeny recapitulating philogeny. On the other hand, Lévi-Strauss's idea that social behavior stems from the elemental (unconscious) rules of culture (the rule of exogamy, the principle of reciprocity, exchange of goods, alliance, etc.) is likewise a variation on the "grounding" importance of individual behavior, which only "has meaning" in the overall context of cultural structures.

We find, therefore, that:

5. $A = C, B = D, A' = B'$ and $C' = D'$
   $A/B, \quad C/D, \quad A'/C' \quad$ and B'/D'

This shows the relevancy of the opposing pairs "individual/group" and "nature/culture" and their systematic relationship to the third pair, ground/grounded. The permutations we have worked out allow us to reconstruct the "semantic field" of a specific set of philosophical problems which goes beyond the individual "choices" of a given philosopher.

3. Philosophy and Its Shadow

The advantages of this method are obvious: they allow us to reconstitute the underlying structure of a set of philosophical discourses which will appear after the analysis to be transformations of a common base. The analysis we have just made is still quite provisional: in no way can we proclaim with certainty that the structural method is fruitful in the area of philosophical and metaphysical systems. Nevertheless, I think it will be interesting to test the hypothesis, as we will certainly make some interesting discovery or other in the process.

Let us, for example, go back to diagram A. We have agreed that it applies to Sartre's early work. We could also apply it to the so-called "subjective idealism" of Fichte. Although this commonly used term was uncritically taken from the philosopher's own statements, it nevertheless has its raison d'être. In order to discover this, however, we must abandon the traditional dichotomy of idealism/realism (or idealism/materialism) so that we can observe, from a distance, how the term appears in Fichte's discourse. In effect, the idealism of the Subject is one of only two paths of reflection identified by Fichte. The other path, which is the opposite of idealism, is *dogmatism*—that is, a philosophy which holds that the ground of consciousness and knowledge is in "things in themselves." This is a philosophy of necessity, in other words, opposed to a philosophy of freedom (idealism), a philosophy which takes the object to be the ground instead of the I.

Let us leave Fichte behind and return to our models. The description of the elements of this philosophy does not allow us to maintain as valid the distinction between natural and social objects at the heart of what is opposed to subjectivity. It is simply the "not-I", that is, any object (natural, cultural, supernatural) which puts up resistance to the I, which sets itself apart from the I. Now, dogmatism turns out to be the exact inversion of this situation, as is any philosophy which raises something which is not the I, something we call a "thing," to the status of "ground." We therefore find that idealism corresponds to diagram A (incorporating C) and that dogmatism corresponds to diagram A' (incorporating C'). It appears that dogmatism refutes the equations and dichotomies that our analysis has developed. Suddenly we have an equation which contradicts the above:

Dogmatism: A' = C' // Freud/Lévi-Strauss: A'/C'

It would appear that we must alter our diagram if we are to make room for dogmatic philosophy. But before we take this drastic step

let us look at this kind of philosophy. To begin with, in which text
or group of texts is dogmatism presented?

Fichte makes references to Spinoza, to the French materialists,
to Berkeley, to Plato . . . on the face of it, a motley and incongruous
group.

Must we discuss all of these references in order to understand
dogmatic philosophy? I don't think that such a massive and ultimately fruitless undertaking is worth the trouble, for a very simple
reason: dogmatism as we have defined it only appears in *one* quite
specific text, that is, in the first introduction to Fichte's *Science of
Knowledge.* Dogmatism is Fichte's own invention. Before him no
one had defined a philosophy in which the human I is derived from
and based on a "non-I" that we call Thing, a philosophy which
continued to consider the pairings human I/Thing, Freedom/Ne-
cessity, Ground/Grounded, etc., to be the relevant terms of philosophical discussion.

But Fichte "keeps" or "chooses" only one of the members of
each "dilemma" or "option." He "marks" one member, withdrawing
or suppressing the other and presenting it as a mere *shadow* or
negative referent.

At this point we discover something surprising: we realize that
Fichte has done nothing less than invent *two philosophies,* the "subjective idealism" which everyone accepts as his *real* philosophy and
dogmatism, the *exact inverse* of Fichte's idealism. It is, in other words,
the *alternative philosophy* lying beneath the system of "binary" options that allows us to *choose* idealism.

Fichte is therefore not an "idealist." For this blindly accepted
commonplace we must substitute a subtler and more accurate as-
sessment. Fichte's discourse signals the emergence of a system of
options which can take the form of both idealism and dogmatism
(rather, diagrams A and A', in which A' is the structural inversion
of A as indicated in diagrams 4 and 4'). Fichte's "conscious" discourse therefore implies that one of the members of each pair of
opposites is "singled out" with the positive sign (+). "Dogmatism,"
for its part, is then the set of (−) options which are thereby elim-

inated. It is that "other discourse" which is withdrawn and "denounced," the *repressed shadow* against which the unambiguous *presence* of a sign can stand out. It is the absent discourse, evoked only in order to be shunned or passed over, which *allows* and *makes possible* the emergence of the *chosen* discourse.

Now, this "shadow" only "appears" if one allows the basic alternative implied by a double series of options. This alternative must be examined in each philosophical system. In Fichte's case we can see that the alternative implied by the series of options is that between ground and grounded in relation to the opposition between I and Thing. It would be worthwhile to discover the fundamental alternatives at work in other systems.

In any event, the model that we initially proposed must be expanded to create room for the "shadows" of the various models as they appear. The important thing to notice is that the realm of these shadows constitutes a model which is the symmetrical inverse of the existing model and that no "shadow" can possibly fit in the original model. The resulting model presents the following equations and oppositions:

6. $A/C, B/D, A'/B', C'/D'$
$A = B, C = D, A' = C', B' = D'$

which is the inverse of diagram 5. It helps us to understand why:

while:

Dogmatism: $A' = C'$ (diagram 6)

Freud/Lévi-Strauss: A'/C' (diagram 5)

It should be clear that this procedure or method, even when applied with a certain playfulness and frivolity, enables us to propose a number of surprising and unexpected working hypotheses which current methodologies could hardly be expected to generate. One of these might be stated in this way: No philosophy is limited to creating the "philosophy" that we commonly associate with a text or group of texts (this is the case, for instance, of Fichte's subjectivism). All philosophies unconsciously create sets of problems and structures which reflect sets of interrelated options. At the same time, each philosophy "chooses" one of the two series of options and raises it to the level of consciousness, repressing the other to the extent that the conscious mind is aware of it only as a *negative referent*. First and foremost, philosophies are related to the very reverse of what they enunciate and unwittingly develop. In this way each philosophy *invents* its own twin, which is what it then *denounces*.

    7. General Diagram:

(+) Philosophies:	$A = C, B = D, A' = B', C' = D'$
	$A/B, C/D, A'/C', B'/D'$
(−) Shadows:	$A/C, B/D, A'/B', C'/D'$
	$A = B, C = D, A' = C', B' = D'$

Conclusion

We began this essay by deploring the sterile denunciations proferred by a number of philosophical schools and tendencies that still command a sizable audience. We called attention to the righteous horror inspired by that something called "metaphysics." We also briefly questioned whether this "obsessive" condemnation might be aimed at a figment of the imagination.

The following essay will show to what extent metaphysics really is a ghost. We can already guess, for the same reason that Fichte's philosophy is "dogmatic," why this might be the case. Metaphysics embraces all discourses which "choose" alternatives that correspond to and "oppose" the alternatives "marked" by logical positivism: *metaphysics is an invention of logical positivism.* If the latter feels it must launch an all-out war against metaphysics it is because it *has* to conjure up this ghost, this shadow: it is the only way logical positivism can "assert," "de-*sign*ate," "de-*mar*cate" itself. Without metaphysics, logical positivism would step from its terra firma into the quicksand of that "Nothingness" which both terrifies and titillates it.

2

The Structure and Function
of Philosophy

WHAT is philosophy? What purpose does it serve? What purpose has it served or will it serve, if it still has any purpose
at all? Is it a nostalgic discourse which longs for a glorious past
while bemoaning the misfortunes of the present? Is it an arrogant
discourse which makes clever use of rhetoric and delivery to mask
a basic lack of substance? Or is it on the contrary a modest analytical
activity which looks into the structure of the various fields of knowledge? Is philosophy nothing more than method, or is it a different
kind of learning, a learning about first principles or fundamentals?
Is it a changeful kind of learning which feeds on incessant self-
criticism, whose mission is to ferret out what is left of "philosophy"
in either the sciences or "praxis"? Is it a discourse which accomplishes its mission by dismantling or destroying itself, or is it a
constantly self-questioning kind of discourse that asks itself, again
and again, "what is philosophy?"

This avalanche of questions is far from exhaustive. It suffices,
however, to show the extent to which puzzlement, ignorance, and
disagreement characterize the "state of the question." Despite a
proliferation of books on the subject, like Ortega's, there has been
no real advance toward providing a definitive answer. Sacristán's
treatment does not satisfy us in this respect either, much less the

articles appearing on the "op-ed" pages of those journals which
currently pontificate on such matters.

Given this state of affairs, is there any value in further clouding
the debate by broadcasting a few observations of a polemical nature? Is it worthwhile, moreover, to go out on a limb in defense
of opinions that are quite hostile to those usually defended with
such zeal in the pages of these journals?

Is it worthwhile to point out that the "latest" cliché—that philosophy, once a fertile dame, is now sterile and exhausted from
giving birth to those strong and robust young women we call the
sciences—is growing tedious by dint of being so often heard, and
the same with all the familiar writing about the "death of speculative
philosophy"? Might it not be more useful to do without these facile,
house-broken attitudes, to approach the problem from a more rigorous, less nineteenth-century point of view?

1. Philosophy as the Semaphore of Knowledge

The question we are raising—"what is philosophy and what is
its function?"—implies a more concrete problem: What discourses,
texts, or forms of expression do we consider "philosophical"? Can
we rightfully use this non-polyvalent term to designate texts apparently as different as Parmenides' poem, Plato's dialogues, Descartes' *Meditations*, Kant's critiques, *The Phenomenology of Mind,
Being and Time* and Popper's *The Logic of Scientific Discovery*? Is it
not foolish to bring all of these texts together under one heading?
Do they really make a single group, be it homogeneous or incongruous? What, if any, is the *common ground* of this group of texts?
What, in fine, is the unity of *philosophical discourse*?

There have been repeated attempts to expose this supposed unity
and to show the extent to which the grouping is totally arbitrary.
Historical reasons are given: one name alone—philosophy—cannot possibly embrace a would-be grouping of such disparate texts.
Or, it is said, only a retrospective "interpretation," from present-
day premises, of texts from the past could possibly justify such a

grouping. Like "literature," "philosophy" could not be used to allude to specific texts so widely separated by time and space and belonging to such irreconcilably different cultural traditions. The continuity suggested by the use of these terms would reveal, upon investigation, a discontinuity among the texts being designated. "Soul," "reason," "being," and "concept" would take on different meanings from one text to the next. A "perennial set of problems" would therefore be difficult to isolate or could be defined only at the risk of doing violence to the texts or making abrasive extrapolations. One would maintain in vain that the "subject-object" problem or the issue of "a priori concepts" can already be seen in Leonardo da Vinci or in Plato. To back up his claim, the interpreter would have to squeeze the text until *he made it say* what in reality it never said. By a marvelous trick of exegesis we can then maintain that while what is said on the surface is one thing and what is "not said" is another, the latter is nevertheless "implicit" in the former. Now, these signs which are added to the text belong in effect to a separate text, the exegete's. The theory of interpretation or commentary assumes that all *signifiers* are elliptical by nature and withdrawn by choice: they always hide an *excess* of meanings, and these emerge gradually with each successive reading. But where does this "excess" exist if not in the reader himself?

Because of its methodological shortcomings, the theory of interpretation does not allow us to find the unity of philosophical problems. For the same reason we cannot strike a compromise with history, hypothesizing the existence of problems that became known in ancient Greece and have been "evolving" ever since. One ends up dissolving the apparent unity of the texts in question. Each of them is cautiously thought to "express" a synthesis of experiences and knowledge or a "world view" characteristic of a given period or culture in the best possible way. Instead of searching for the unity of philosophy in its history, thereby avoiding the danger of dissolving the whole into a multitude of monadic "bodies" with neither doors nor windows, we relate these discourses to mythical, literary, and political discourse—that is, to the totality of practical pursuits that constitute the patrimony of a given period or culture.

When we take this dramatic step, however, we are suddenly lost in Schelling's dark night where all cats are black.

In this way more or less cautious and plausible answers are given to the problem of the unity of philosophy. They vacillate between totally negating and unconditionally affirming this unity. Rarely, however, do we find an even minimally rigorous *criterion* by which to enlighten the questioner. And to the extent that we leave the question floating in the air we insure the continuation of an especially picturesque tradition of speculation—the philosophical tradition—whose object of study is nothing other than "searching for philosophy." The philosopher's specialty is in effect the search for his own specialty. This circularity is justified by an authorized and consecrated Text: it was Aristotle who said that metaphysics is science in search of itself.

Will we once and for all stop looking for a line of reasoning that authorizes us to lump these texts together under the same name? Will we finally stop talking about "philosophy" when we refer to these texts as a whole and restrict our use of the term to a specific text, according to our private taste and judgment? The only way to resist these tempting alternatives is to discover a unified *set of problems* in what is usually called the "history of philosophy." We must locate a common *underlying structure* in texts from both the past and the future which remains the same throughout a period of time. We must be able to identify a *perennial problem* common to all of these discourses.

Does a problem with these characteristics exist? Can we find its monotonous, always unquestioning presence in a group of so-called philosophical texts?

We will attempt to resolve this difficulty by proposing a working hypothesis derived from a number of specialized studies that verify or disprove the hypothesis or concretely identify the group of texts for which it is valid. This hypothesis is intended to clarify this matter once and for all. The present essay will be limited to describing the means by which the investigation should be carried out.

We are affirming nothing more nor less than the unity and "perennial" nature of the problems addressed by philosophical discourse. We believe in effect that we can discover a common, unchanging set of problems, or rather a single problem, ranging from Parmenides' poem—or more specifically from Socrates' question to Theaetetus: "What is knowledge?" (ti episteme?)—to Carnap's discourse on overcoming metaphysics. Following Popper, we propose to call this problem the "problem of demarcation."[1] We are convinced that it appears over and over again in this "succession" of texts and that it confers a special identity and unity to philosophical discourse.

The fact that these problems continue to crop up is proven by some of the articles that appear on the latest "op-ed" pages. If we know how to read them, we see that they are restating the problem of demarcation. These discourses, although hot off the press, are still *philosophical* in the rustiest and most outdated sense of the word. They are the latest "survivals" of a set of problems dating back historically to the founding of Attica. Underlying them is a *structure* which gives them meaning and integrates them into a tradition thousands of years old. It is precisely this archaic quality that we want to capture in this essay.

Let us suppose, for instance, that scientific discourse is set apart from other kinds of discourse because it fulfills certain requirements—symbolic clarity, logical consistency and the possibility of verifying its claims—which are related to a *set of rules*. Granted these premises, we can identify those discourses in which these traits are *present* or *absent*. We might distinguish the "empirical sciences," for instance, in which all three requirements are met, from the "formal sciences," which meet the first two. We can now call this common denominator the *mark of scientificity*. With it we can draw a box divided into two compartments: the right-hand compartment contains those discourses in which the mark is present (*marked* discourses). In the left-hand compartment we will place those discourses which in fact or in theory lack this same mark (*unmarked* discourses), although they may eventually acquire the mark. We can therefore differentiate between two general categories of discourse: "scientific" discourses and "literary" discourses.

Carnap, for one, presents a box with these characteristics. The difference is that he adds a third, central compartment between the other two. It contains hybrid discourses ($\pm$) showing both the provisional presence and the provisional absence of the mark. The right-hand compartment is full of marked disciplines: physics, chemistry, biology, and the hard sciences. Literature, that is, discourse in which the mark is absent ($-$), occupies the left-hand compartment. In the central compartment are the so-called "human sciences" (psychology and sociology), in which the mark is partially present in certain branches of study and absent from others either because they are "literary" in nature or because their statements are still "ambiguous." Metaphysics is situated in this central compartment. But whereas the human sciences tend toward the "right," metaphysics, despite the fact that it would like to pass for a science of the same caliber as the hard sciences, in fact leans toward the left-hand compartment. Carnap examines Heidegger's statements about "nothingness" in these terms, revealing the extent to which they break the rules governing the generation of meaningful statements. These kinds of discourse must expose their embarrassing ambiguity and be classified as tending toward the right ($\rightarrow$) or toward the left ($\leftarrow$). The human sciences tend toward the scientific community, but metaphysics has meaning only as a literary discourse which, like literature, translates "affective states"[2] (see figure 2.1).

Let us for the moment design our *hypothesis* to fit this single example. Carnap's discourse thus serves as a "referential myth" like the Bororo myth of the "dénicheur d'oiseaux" (o xibae e iari).[3] Further on, in chapter 3, we will add a summary of other, apparently different philosophical discourses and demonstrate that the same formal structure reappears in them all.

Carnap's discourse enables us to perform the following *operation*: taking as a basis the square with three compartments (figure 2.1)

Figure 2.1

(−)	(±)	(+)
Literature	$\rightarrow$ Human sciences $\leftarrow$ Metaphysics	Sciences

we *empty* it of its *contents* (science/metaphysics/literature, etc.), in-
terpreting these contents as *variables*. We also interpret the actual
rules which define the degree of scientificity as variables in which
x, y, and z are variables (see figure 2.2).

This operation allows us at last to state our hypothesis: Is the
square with its three compartments and their corresponding *signs*
not an enduring constant? Does it not appear over and over again
in a variety of discourses from Parmenides and Plato to Carnap?
Is not the perennial problem of philosophy perhaps the task of
filling this box with specific contents corresponding to the varying
sets of rules adopted by each philosophy?

We have already given this problem the name of demarcation.
According to this hypothesis each philosophy in effect defines its
unique task as that of visibly *marking* those discourses *marked as
knowledge* by a specific set of rules. By extension, each philosophy
de-marcates those (−) discourses in which the mark is absent. All
philosophies therefore raise a question which is predicated on
maintaining this configuration (figure 2.2), the true *structure* of
philosophical discourse. And each philosophy answers the question

Figure 2.2

(−)	(±)	(+)
x	$\leftarrow$ y $\rightarrow$	z

in its *own* way, in accordance with the (variable) set of rules it adopts. The box outlined in figure 2.2 represents this structure.

Of course we are looking at this structure in its purely *formal* aspect, after the contents have been removed and the *modality* of the set of rules adopted or instituted by any given philosophy has been set aside. Does it not for precisely this reason constitute the *form* which in some way or another *informs* all philosophical discourse? Is philosophy—that is, reflection about knowledge, the answer to Socrates' "ti episteme?"—not then a discourse whose *problems* always assume this configuration? Is the diagram in question perhaps the *commonplace*, the *topos* that congeals philosophy, giving it both unity and specificity throughout what appears to be its history? Is not the task of all philosophy to give an accounting of the problem of demarcation, that is, in some fashion to fill the various compartments, thereby distributing the various *signs* among the contents that pertain to each specific case?

Philosophy consequently is structured like a traffic light or semaphore, the semaphore of knowledge which gives the "green light" to certain (+) discourses, "letting them through," clearing the way for other discourses to ascend to the compartment of science by flashing the yellow that goes before the green (→). It also slows the progress of various "pseudosciences," clearing the way for their entrance into the compartment of *non-science*, flashing the yellow that precedes the red (←). Finally, it stops clearly "unmarked" discourses with the red light (−). Philosophy, the semaphore of knowledge, allows science to circulate freely while detaining all candidates who do not possess the *mark* required by science.

2. Philosophy and the Baptism of Knowledge

Philosophy's function in regard to knowledge has long been debated. The question has often been asked: What does philosophy *add* to the sciences, what gap does it bridge in the area of human understanding? And the answer has often been given that *philosophy adds nothing to science*, that it is not a discipline in competition with science, that it does not therefore deal in scientific facts. The debate closes with the conclusion that philosophy is merely a *means of analyzing* science, a tool for studying the logic and methodology of science.

Here, however, we make a larger claim. Certainly philosophy is—as it has been!—a means of analyzing the sciences which allows us to clarify scientific statements and procedures. It is a reflection on the various fields of knowledge or, as Popper says, it is the theory of theories.[4] It is the "science of the sciences" not in the sense of a "queen" of science but rather of a *metalanguage* whose *language-object* is the sciences. In this respect philosophy definitely does not add anything to science but merely clarifies it.

From our point of view, however, we can state that philosophy adds something to science. As we have seen, it adds the (+) sign by which science is *marked* and *demarcated*, by contrast to something we can now call *non-science*. Philosophy adds to science precisely the *name* of science.

Philosophy does not simply analyze. In fact it fulfills a more ancient, fundamental, and characteristic function: it legislates and differentiates. It makes the traffic stop and go: it is the semaphore of knowledge. Philosophy is that discourse which asks King Solomon's question: Whose is the child? and like him decides whether the child belongs to the community of sciences or to the dark recesses where the non-sciences abide. Philosophy has a *ritual* function: it gives names to discourses, calling them *sciences*. It also creates a *split* in the very heart of human knowledge, which before its intervention is in an "anarchic" state, subject to merely implicit rules. Philosophy creates the *split* between *scientific knowledge* and the pseudosciences or non-sciences. Thanks to philosophy the *neutral* term 'knowledge' or 'science' (which we use when we speak of "Babylonian" or "astrological science") acquires a connotation which blossoms in the apparently redundant expression "scientific knowledge." But, as in the case of the "Coffee Café," it is not really redundant: although it seems one might confuse the second signifier with the first, in fact it has its own value in the syntagmatic chain, a value which is added to the value of the first signifier. It tells us nothing less than that the neutrality of knowledge has given way to *marked knowledge*. The second signifier expresses the sign that philosophy adds to neutral knowledge, the sign connoted by the terms 'science' and 'knowledge' once philosophy has acquitted them of all charges—that is, once the problem of demarcation or the *ritual of marking* has been undertaken. It is the mark which raised knowledge to the status of having the *name* of knowledge.

For this reason philosophy is a ritual: it names, *baptizes*, de-*sig*-*na*tes, calls things by *new* names. Like Yahweh with Adam, philosophy expresses, with a new sign, a *change of surroundings* with regard to knowledge. It adds the supernatural to nature; it drops a sign into the gray monotony of knowledge. It carves its name in the flesh of certain sciences and draws a line between the (+) and (−) zones of neutral knowledge. Philosophy thus marks and sets science apart from non-science, enacting a ritual ceaselessly pursued by the good historian and the ethnologist: the ritual which establishes a zone of *inclusion* and a zone of *exclusion*. Philosophy *creates* the structure of inclusion and exclusion within the realm of science, or, as we shall see later, *philosophy allows this structure to emerge in the domain of the sciences*.

From this follows a great number of consequences. One of them, perhaps the most serious, is the immediate repercussion on the sciences, which are *transformed* to the extent that the structure of inclusion and exclusion, thanks to philosophy, becomes clear in their domain. Science is no longer "free," restricted by immanent norms alone. From now on science is only called by this name once it has submitted itself to the proof of demarcation. From the moment philosophy comes into its own, science is both linked to and cut off from that "other" kind of knowledge—non-science—which philosophy refuses to honor with the consecrated name. By the same token it is also possible to differentiate between two general types of knowledge: *pre-philosophical* (or post-philosophical) knowledge, in which the inclusion/exclusion paradigm does not appear, and the other kind of knowledge in which the split is effective, creating the duality of science and "pseudoscience."

In this way structural analysis enables us to get the upper hand in regard to the nagging question about the *origin* of philosophy. It is said that structural analysis cannot account for generation when in fact it enables us to find a rigorous criterion for establishing *when* philosophy comes into being. We now know that this event is simultaneous with the birth of that kind of knowledge that is differentiated from other kinds of knowledge, which it banishes. Philosophy is born at that moment when, like Parmenides, we are warned to avoid certain directions of inquiry.

At the same time our analysis puts us on the trail of the even more surprising discovery that a *new* science, a *different kind of knowledge*, is born with philosophy: science characterized by the structure of inclusion and exclusion.

Before we go on to refine these insights, however, we must specify the *means* we will use to prove our hypothesis. This will consist primarily of summarizing other texts and philosophical discourses (figure 2.1). It is not actually a proof so much as a series of brief suggestions intended to lead to a proof. A rigorous demonstration would require a narrow and detailed study which is quite far from our present purpose.

3. Philosophy in the Plural

Let us now assume that there is a set of rules which all learned discourses follow in *defining* and *classifying* names that refer to forms already assumed to be real (ideas). This discourse should above all define, de-limit, and ascertain the precise boundaries of each form, showing the *differences* and *commonalities* that unite or separate the forms. It should then go on to classify the ideas thus defined, indicating which can and which cannot combine with others. For example, the form "rest" combines with the form "being," to which the form "movement" also corresponds. While "rest" and "movement" correspond in this respect, in other respects they differ. The learned man—the dialectician—will therefore note the "natural connections" between the forms, focusing on subtle distinctions that usually go undetected. He will, in other words, use an *ascending* method which enables him to move from the plurality of forms to that single idea that depends on no other (anhypotheton) as well as a *descending* method by which he articulates the invisible ideas and the "ideal" atoms (atoma eide).[5]

Once we have established these premises we can expose those discourses which consistently tend to confuse the names of things, defining or classifying them inappropriately, blocking the natural connections between the forms, and uttering "nonsense" like "rest and movement are the same in all respects." The *sophist*, who contradicts everything, is the "antilogos" of this prosecution. He is the original precedent of the modern "metaphysician," defined as a "creator of illusions" who manufactures scientific mirages— the genuine play-actor of science. Like the metaphysician in other prosecutions, the sophist *passes himself off as a learned man without actually being one.* Sophistry and its techniques (eristics and rhetoric) constitute the *relevant pseudoscience* of this prosecution, as they set out to compete with dialectics. The philosopher—legislator of language, episteme, and polis—marks it with the yellow light that comes before the "red." Eristics and rhetoric thus tend toward that dark area reserved by the "non-sciences."

Through the Stranger, Plato thus completes, in the *Sophist*, the set of rules sketched in the *Meno* and the *Phaedrus*. The *Sophist* in effect fully answers Socrates' question in the *Theaetetus*: "What is knowledge?" (*ti episteme?*). With this question the set of philosophical questions breaks forth in an *explicit, thematic* fashion. The *Sophist* makes it quite clear that the answer can only be made once knowledge has been *demarcated* to differentiate it from what it most closely resembles while standing nevertheless at the farthest distance, namely, sophistry. This can be accomplished only when the set of rules that enables us finally to "locate" science and sophistry has been put in place and the corresponding signs distributed between them. The *Theaetetus* merely sets the stage for this: it is a disturbing dialogue because it tells us what knowledge is *not* instead of what it is. It identifies what knowledge *can* but *should not* be mistaken for. Three hypotheses about the nature of knowledge are suggested in this dialogue, but they are all rejected, after being subjected to an exhaustive analysis. The first hypothesis states that knowledge is not aesthesis or sensual perception; the second, that it is not *ortha doxa*, that is, just opinion. Neither is it "just opinion allied with reason." In this way Plato clears the way that will lead him, in the *Sophist*, to identify knowledge in the true sense of the word, that is, knowledge of the ideas used by dialectics (+). Opinion or *doxa* is by contrast the (±) intermediary between *episteme* and *amathia*, between science and non-science, by virtue of its double identity as just (→) or "plausible" (reasonable, "acceptable") opinion and *false* (←) *opinion* as well. The latter is usually the domain of the sophist.

In any case, opinion occupies the middle ground between knowledge and base ignorance. At the end of Book V of the *Republic*, Plato arranges science, opinion, and "non-science" in a tripartite hierarchy. *For the first time in history Plato thus draws the formal diagram of the code of philosophical discourse* (see figure 2.2 above).

As we shall see in chapter 7, Plato follows a very subtle and sophisticated procedure in establishing this set of rules. Socrates in effect takes shelter behind a wall of *docta ignorantia* which enables him to analyze the issue at hand—knowledge—in great detail. His questioning implies a distanced indifference toward the object of the inquiry. It implies a highly developed consciousness of philosophical problems.

In Parmenides' poem, on the other hand, we find a simple, straightforward, immediate statement of a set of rules. We might say that it erupts unconsciously or semiconsciously. These problems are first stated *consciously* with Plato's question, *ti episteme?*

And yet in Parmenides' poem we already find the *condition of possibility* of this question. For the first time it is publicly stated that one should not follow a certain path of investigation, that one should avert one's eyes from that road. The light is on red in that direction, while the go-ahead has been given to the one legitimate discourse—that which repeats again and again, ceaselessly pounding in the message, that "things *are*." This is the discourse which enunciates the true, tautological sphere of being. It also points to a "third way," the way of opinion which is midway between the way of truth and the way of falsehood. This third way enables us to make plausible statements about appearances ($\rightarrow$), but it can also lead to the error of those who think that "the way to all things goes in opposite directions" ($\leftarrow$).

The *underlying structure* of philosophical discourse thus appears for the first time in this poem. This structure is the true *historical a priori* of philosophy: it gives unity and specificity to philosophical problems and guarantees their historical dimension. It is not merely a conglomeration of parts or pieces: like Minerva, it is born fully grown. In this sense philosophy is a *break with* and a *qualitative leap beyond* previous types of knowledge. Philosophy relocates the very ground of knowledge, promoting it to a higher level (with no implications of "improvement" or progress, however). Philosophy converts "free," "pre-philosophical" knowledge, subject only to internal or implicit norms, into a science sundered from non-science, a science divided into "marked" knowledge and pseudoscience. We might say, paraphrasing Nietzsche, that Discernment begins with philosophy (the capital D denotes the added sign). With philosophy (exchanging a capital S for capital D), *incipit Sapientiam!*

It is no accident that a Goddess communicates these secrets and mysteries of Science to the mortals, as all of the "highest values" (in the Nietzschean sense) come from "on high." Just as morality had its Moses, philosophy's Sinai is in Parmenides. This philosophical Moses *received* the tablets of the laws of knowledge fully saddled and ready to ride. A supplementary domain then *rode on top of* the implicit domain of knowledge, just as the Commandments were *added* to the implicit domain of social institutions.

From Parmenides to Carnap philosophy has had a fully sacred and ritual connotation. Every time a philosopher *recreates* the tablets in their formal aspect he experiences a thrill that carries him back to the *beginning*, to that moment masterfully played and recorded by Parmenides, when he says: "the goddess treated me kindly." All "archeology of knowledge" must therefore begin with this Poem. Although it seems hard to believe, Parmenides' poem is not legendary but *historical*. This is the advantage that the archeology of knowledge has over psychoanalysis: while the latter must construe the roots of the individual and social strife which characterizes all psychic existence by recourse to a *creation myth*, the archeology of knowledge has a *creation myth* which is also a document. It need not invent the proof, as Freud had to do in *Totem and Taboo*: it need only analyze it.

Let us now take for granted that in the final analysis all sciences are nothing but "human discernment," and that this is nourished by certain "seeds" or "spontaneous truths" which have the same substance, nature, and essence as Reason and which manifest themselves clearly to Reason if it remains alert, refusing to be distracted by "hasty and groundless" conjectures.[6] In order to proceed knowledgeably *now*, we must follow the four rules established by the method. We must obey certain representations or simple "ideas" which bear the mark of self-evidence. We must necessarily begin with our intuition of these "clear and distinct" ideas in order to move on, later, by gradual, systematic *deduction*, to less evident representations deriving from those others. It is necessary, therefore, to go from the simple to the complex, from the obvious to the less obvious.

Any discourse which does not proceed in this manner will be guilty of proceeding *unsystematically*, either because it errs by beginning with more complex, less obvious issues which it *attempts to pass off* as simple issues (scholastic philosophy commits this error) or because instead of relating the representations in question in terms of equality and inequality, it relies on "affinities," "sympathies" or "analogies" (*mauvaises doctrines* like magic and astrology). Descartes, in reviewing the state of the sciences, exiled all of these "sciences," along with theology, to the region of non-science, because they all present knowledge that surpasses the limited powers of human reason. Above all he renounces the *pseudoscience* of scholasticism, which attempts to answer all kinds of questions without taking into account the limitations of human reason and its self-made counterbalance, skepticism (that is, the kind of knowledge that renounces itself when it discovers its own illusory nature [←]). Descartes on the other hand tried to raise to the level of science all kinds of disciplines still characterized by methodological chaos and doubt, disciplines like mathematics (which he himself practiced), medicine, and physics (→).

Let us now consider that the true knowledge of things must take into account certain "conditions of possibility." Let us further establish certain a priori forms of intuition and certain categories of human understanding as these conditions. Under these conditions alone can we make judgments that aspire to objectivity. If a judgment is not based on a previous a priori intuition of the forms "space" and "time," it is merely analytical: it cannot make a "transcendent use" of these forms. Scientific judgments, however, are synthetic: in them the predicate adds something to the subject. They are broad judgments, and they add to our knowledge of things.[7]

By this criterion only certain sciences are correctly named. In effect, Newton's physical mathematics alone creates this kind of judgment. When we say that the sum of the angles of a triangle is equal to the sum of two right angles or that a straight line is the shortest distance between two points we are in effect basing our judgment on a spatial representation. Similarly, when we say that two and two are four we are basing our judgment on a sequential representation of numbers in time. These kinds of judgments, characteristic of the sciences just mentioned, therefore enter into the community of *marked discourses*. Metaphysics, on the other hand, does not create this kind of judgment—and yet metaphysics presents itself as the queen and arbiter of all knowledge. If we examine metaphysical judgments, however, we find that they are paralogical, that they lead to unsolvable antinomies. This is because metaphysical judgments characteristically rely on the "improper use of categories," a use which goes "beyond the limits and conditions of human experience." In fact, it is an abuse. Metaphysics owes its "illusory" character to this abuse, in which it is aided and abetted by the "illusion of transcendence." Critical philosophy should take it upon itself to expose this typically intellectual illusion whenever it fails to result in a "transcendental reflection" on its own conditions and limitations. *Dialectics*, in this sense, is that branch of philosophy in charge of revealing metaphysics' illusory nature and vain pretension of passing itself off as a science (←). Metaphysics should be denounced by the prosecution of philosophy (critical philosophy) as a pseudoscience that tends to set forth on a "shadowy ocean" where Reason goes astray and, once it has gone beyond its own limitations, dissipates and disappears. In this way metaphysics leads to "non-science."

Let us now imagine a set of rules which stipulates that true knowledge be based on a solid *ground* (*Grund*) from which it is possible to *deduce* the entire *system of knowledge*. The rules stipulate that this ground be the *Self's reflection on itself*. In order to earn the name, every science must be based on or presuppose this primordial reflection. How can we understand an object if we do not already know something about the observing "subject" who constitutes the very condition of possibility of the object's manifestation as an object? We must understand this subject who is the ground and criterion of objectivity. Consequently, any science which is not based on this understanding must be expelled from the "system of science," for it will be *dogmatic* science that elevates the "thing in itself" rather than its opposite, the Self, as the ground or condition of possibility.[8]

Discourses which in their heyday belonged to the community of the sciences will now fall under the category of "dogmatism" (that is, the non-science relevant to this prosecution). Among them we will find such enterprises as Berkeley and the materialists, Wolff's old school and several aspects of Kantianism. This may strike us today as a motley, incongruous whole, but in their time they were regarded—by Fichte—as a homogeneous group: he noticed that all of them lacked a mark.

Finally, trembling with apprehension, let us put an end to all this philosophical rigamarole and ready the "unformed individual" for his initiation into an absolute Science which recapitulates all "philosophies" (that is, philosophical tendencies), developing them all simultaneously and revealing their "momentous" truth.[9] To this end we will persist in questioning naive consciousness until we have freed it from appearances and introduced it to that empyrean of pure essences wherein dwells the Mind-in-and-for-itself. Knowledge is here defined as Mental consciousness, as the conceptual revelation of its substance, as spiritual substance finally transformed into subjectivity—or if you wish, as spiritual subjectivity finally transformed into substance. . . . This voracious Science, which Hegel likens to a bacchanalian frenzy, devours all of the truths of the past and turns them all into facets of its own spiritual organism, at the same time killing the all-embracing appetite of each part of the consciousness. Absolute Knowledge can only be attained by universalizing all of these "refuted" figures through the painful enactment of each necessary instance. This is the true Calvary and the bitter cup of the Mind. Absolute Knowledge is the *memory* of these eclipsed images and their melancholy, twilight absorption into concepts.

In this prosecution Knowledge has therefore been defined as the demonstration of the substance of the mind in the form of concepts. It banishes from knowledge any incomplete grasp of that substance which aspires to universality. This aspiration will be exposed and refuted in its *incompleteness* (that is, the non-science pertaining to this prosecution). All of the figures of consciousness will thus be revealed as aspiring to *stop* the dialectical process and "plan" how to attain an absolute Truth which phenomenological analysis discovers to be *abstract*. It will become clear that these aspirations to truth are mere *opinions* and that, as such, they will both be eliminated from science—and the "appearance" that they create (←) will thereby be destroyed—and also be *maintained* once the progress of the dialectic (→) has surpassed them.

Philosophies are constantly trying to state and solve the nagging problem of demarcation, and the *divided box* constantly reappears as the *condition of possibility* of solving the problem. Different philosophies may "fill" the compartments with different contents or distribute the same contents in a different order, putting them in this compartment or that, but the basic *diagram* remains the same. Each philosophy brings a different set of rules into play, stating the same problem in a different *way*. But *as sets of problems, all philosophies are effectively the same, differing in their means of approach.* Whence the paradox of philosophical discourse: it is monotonously repetitious but gives the impression of the babblings of so many madmen.

As sets of problems, then, all philosophies are the same. In this sense, it does not change from Parmenides to Carnap. For this very reason it can be studied *synchronically*. Throughout what appears to be its history (which is only real at the level of its "contents," so to speak) we see a recurrent and unchanging structure. This structure was sketched by Plato and Carnap, among others, although they lacked the necessary *distance* to understand what they were doing. Of them we might say, paraphrasing Marx, that they may not know what they are doing, but they are *doing* it all the same.[10] For one thing, they created and re-created the structure that give unity and coherence to philosophical discourse. For another, they gave science a new connotation. This connotation worked a transformation, enabling it to change from "free" knowledge to sundered knowledge bearing the brand of Western thought—branded, that is, as we shall see in chapter 12, by the structure of inclusion and exclusion.

This is why philosophy *does not change*. It cannot change without ceasing to be what it is. Regardless of the fuss and gibberish of logical positivism and analytical philosophy, philosophy never has been and never will be *revolutionary*. A genuine revolution would *swallow* philosophy up, in effect clearing the way for a new, free science in which no kinds of discourse were forbidden and no "paths of inquiry" were blocked. Philosophy can only aspire to *reform*. All of its "revolutions" rest on the same, enduring structure. Only the modality varies, that is, the way in which each individual instance arranges the materials within the box. The form stays the same: only the contents change. The problem of demarcation is always with us. Only the solutions change.

4. Everyone Is at War

Regarded in this light philosophy can be seen to unite tremendous inflexibility and a wide range of free activity. We might say that although philosophy might strike us as arbitrary in regard to its content, it is nevertheless *formally codified*. This is merely an illusion, however, which we will attempt to dispel in the following essay. Because despite the variations of content we still find an *order of occurrence* operative at the level of the contents.

Let us in the present essay put the contents aside, however, as we are only interested in demonstrating the unity of philosophical discourse, and this is apparent in its *form*. In any event, this form is the deepest, most elementary level of philosophical discourse. In a sense it is its deep underlying structure, the condition of possibility of whatever order we discover to be its *modality*. It is also its most archaic level, in both the historical and the structural sense (we are already beginning to suspect that history and structure mutually require each other). And for this very reason this level of philosophical discourse resists analysis and is never discussed.

Now, the apparent freedom of the contents of philosophical discourse leads us once again to repeat the old notion that philosophers can never come to an agreement. This is only partially true. We might well reply, "In fact, they understand each other quite well in their own way." They understand each other because, in one way or another, they are attacking the same problem. To the extent that each philosophy solves the problem in its own way they

do not understand each other. This is why a number of philosophies, each of which proposes a different set of rules, giving the
green and red lights to different and even opposing contents, can
exist in the same time and place. For Carnap, "existential analysis"
would clearly be a literary discourse, along with metaphysics. For
Heidegger, a science which does not begin with an analysis of
"Dasein" cannot understand anything at all: it is a mindless beast
that exhausts itself stating banalities. "Analytical thinking" would
label "dialectics" a form of "metaphysics," unless it interpreted
dialectics as "analytical thought in action." In Engels' version, "dialectical thinking" labels any nondialectical science as "metaphysical" and "abstract." In both instances metaphysics is understood
to mean a kind of science which does not deserve the name either
because it is "senseless" (logical positivism) or because it is "arti-
ficial" and consequently does not reveal the contradictory nature
of things (Engels). The various philosophies therefore *neutralize*
each other. Everyone is at war. But as in every battle, both sides
are fighting for the same thing. All philosophies do battle in order
to solve the same problem, the problem of demarcation.

   In the midst of the fray the philosophies of yesteryear, with all
their arrogance, are assigned now and again to the dark corner of
non-science. This happens to scholasticism in Descartes' discourse,
to Descartes in Kant's discourse, to Kant in Hegel's, to Hegel in
Feuerbach's, to Feuerbach in Marx's. It happens to "traditional
ontology" in Heidegger's discourse and to Heidegger in Carnap's
and to Carnap in Heidegger's. . . . But the same *space*, divided into
compartments, remains the same in the midst of all this noisy
activity. It lives on even though the *furniture* it contains shifts back
and forth from one area to the next or is substituted by other, more
modern or "functional" pieces. Philosophers are both the sole *users*
of the space and the interior decorators who arrange the floorspace
of given *infrastructures*. For them this space is "underfoot," so to
speak: it antedates them and makes them possible. In some way
it is the a priori of philosophy.

   It might be objected that all of this is too "obvious." But it is
often forgotten precisely because it is so obvious. As Ortega y
Gasset would say, it is the *previous order of beliefs which is taken for*

granted.[11] Yes, we already know that philosophy should demarcate science from non-science, etc., etc. . . . We know all about it, and for this reason we go on "demarcating" without really *thinking* about what we are doing. We know that, as Popper confesses, once we delve into philosophical problems we will come across the problem of demarcation.[12] We know this as assuredly as we know that there is a street on the other side of the front door. But we here maintain, with Ortega, that because we know this so well, because we have found the street every time we have opened the door, we no longer *think* about it any more. Just imagine for a moment that the street is no longer there. All of our mental assumptions might well break down, and at that point we would begin to *think* about the street. The same holds true for this a priori of philosophical discourse. It is a given. We are in the habit of not thinking about it. It belongs to the realm of *unthought* things. And what is not thought about, as Foucault correctly points out, is what is really important in human thought: it is what investigators really ought to look into.[13] If, today, we *can think about the unthought areas of philosophy* it is because we can speculate about the possible *absence* of its structure, because we can imagine what would happen if science—and language in general—were not constrained by a *supercodification* riding herd over its implicit realm. We are beginning to feel that these orders against trodding certain paths, these Wittgensteinian epigrams suggesting we pass over things in repressive silence, carry the weight of an official ban. We begin to wonder what a free culture would be like in which those sciences for centuries inhibited by the prosecution of Western thought were free to express themselves again. In this culture the *mauvaises doctrines* would once again be present, and the *shadows* conjured and exorcised by Cartesian meditations—the madman, the dreamer, the laughing God—would return to our world and speak to us, sharing with us their dangerous knowledge.[14]

Dreams? Utopias? A distinct possibility? I'm not sure. But I do sense that these categories are no longer valid. In any event I sense that today we can think seriously about a culture in which the *structure of inclusion and exclusion* does not stigmatize science like a parasitical second nature that has become identical with its host. Today it is possible to distinguish between knowledge and the supernatural aspect that philosophy has added to knowledge to such an extent that philosophy has mistaken the supernatural for its very substance. For this reason it is possible to *conceive of* the structure that has made this adhesion possible.

To think *what has not been thought*, as we are doing here, is a task fraught with danger. It turns out that the obvious is not so obvious after all. What was once familiar becomes distant and strange. The sciences of culture today constantly gravitate toward this kind of inquiry. They look at Western culture, our own culture, with ethnological eyes, hoping to unearth its unconscious patterns and mechanisms. Ever since Nietzsche, ethnology has turned its attention to the Western culture that gave it birth. What it attempts to bring to light are its own age-old preconceptions. A simple comparison of these preconceptions with those of other cultures brings about a constant reduction of what is most obvious and familiar. This kind of comparison comes to the fore when one tries to analyze the *höchste Werte*, the "highest values" of Western culture. No wonder that Nietzsche, with his customary clairvoyance, considered "philosophy" one of these highest values.[15] Comparing our "Western culture" to others we find a startling difference: in the others, one can scarcely say that *philosophy* exists at all (the exceptions of course merit study). The science developed by those cultures does not have the unusual aspect of Western philosophy, that is, a philosophy split into the two areas of (included) "scientific knowledge" and (excluded) "pseudoscience."

5. Philosophy's Policing Function

Philosophy, the semaphore of knowledge, appears to evolve into a kind of *superstructure* erected on top of knowledge. It is to science what law is to social institutions, morality to social mores, and theology to religion. It is in the nature of philosophy to prosecute, showing the coherence of science on the one hand while establishing certain norms on the other, differentiating between what is allowed and what is forbidden. These norms vary and change, just as the law changes due to the mobility of social institutions and classes and the groups that are in power. It is a "functional" aspect of the forces of hegemony, and when it ceases to act as such a substitute is found. The same thing happens in philosophy with regard to knowledge. It is a function of the "hegemonizing sciences," and when it ceases to play this role it must either be replaced or allowed to endure in the form of a residue or "survivor." This is why philosophy frequently finds it necessary to sanction the laws currently in force and eliminate those which are not conducive to hegemony. It also explains why philosophy, like the law and the entire world of superstructures, tends to share their inertia and give evidence of enormous remaining "residues." The hegemonizing process can for this reason actually coexist with residual processes which have outlived their usefulness. We can thus explain how a kind of philosophy that served a "function" in the (+) science of the Trivium and Quadrivium endures under certain circumstances. Marx's idea of incorporating philosophy as a kind of "ideological superstructure" or "form of consciousness" is for this reason especially successful as long as philosophy is understood to be the superstructure of knowledge and not that of the "economic base."

Philosophy and philosophers are the "watchdogs" of science, in the Platonic sense. In any event, their function is to police. If we are to solve the problem of philosophy's usefulness or uselessness we must first answer the question of whether or not this policing activity is required. "For the time being," however, we will leave this question aside.

The fact that philosophy is actually part of the superstructure explains why, as Hegel brilliantly remarked, philosophy always comes on the scene too late. In fact Hegel goes so far as to say that the owl of Minerva spreads it wings only with the falling of dusk, when life is over and the sky has faded to a dull gray.[16] Philosophy always comes on the scene too late to raise "to the conceptual level" that which has already been spontaneously created or to *propound* what is already accepted, if only unconsciously: that is, what is known without the *consciousness* that it is known. Philosophy may be this very same consciousness, this science in some sense *redundant*, which endows spontaneous knowledge with *consciousness* and a *name*. This is why, like the law, it has a twilight quality to it: because it always comes on the scene too late. The law comes on the scene when the ruling group or class has imposed its reign by force and organized society in its own image, according to its own judgment. Philosophy *rides astride* the theoretical revolutions which create the sciences. Its prospective range is in this sense quite limited. In this respect we agree with Foucault that Bopp, Couvier, and Smith are the revolutionaries and not Kant, Hegel, et alia.[17] Foucault's statement is ambiguous, however, for the simple reason that it allows philosophy to be classified as an analytical investigation of knowledge and science, and as such it could become yet another scientific discipline. Kant, for instance, could be added to the first list of names. In another sense, however, Foucault's statement is correct, because in its capacity of semaphore of knowledge philosophy assumes that those sciences to which it gives the green light or the red have already acquired a shape and definition. What we are saying is that philosophy is now and always has been an analytical discipline, but that it *also* has been and *still is* a form of judicial consciousness and that as such it is a late and apparently superfluous endeavor. But of course it is not superfluous: it adds something to science. It gives it a name.

In this respect we disagree with Foucault's assertion that philosophies are usually "superficial" manifestations pertinent to the study of *doxography* but totally lacking in *archeological* interest. Of course Foucault is right in making this claim within the framework he establishes. Indeed, philosophies do not tend and have not tended to play a leading role in bringing about changes in the various "epistemological fields." Philosophies have always been carried along, in this sense, by the "chain" of revolutions which among other things have determined, in Foucault's opinion, the switch from the "old" to the present-day episteme. The philosophies of Life, Work and Language, as well as the analytical philosophies of existence and mortality, can be possible only under certain epistemological conditions which are *directly* linked to those scientific revolutions that have given rise to disciplines like "political economics," "biology," and "comparative historical grammar." We are not proposing, of course, to evaluate the impressive working hypothesis of *The Order of Things* in these pages. But we can state that at least in some respects philosophy does have genuine archeological relevance. We have already seen how this is so, in our account of Parmenides' poem: philosophy directs us toward a profound transformation of knowledge. From "free knowledge," science becomes a kind of knowledge that is sundered from nonscience. In this respect philosophy brings to light a *deep structure* which acts on and alters the totality of philosophy. This structure is deeper and more ancient than Foucault's "episteme" for two reasons: because it *affects* all of the "epistemes" examined by archeology and because it also precedes them in history. The discovery of this structure also allows us to avoid a major difficulty of *The Order of Things*, that is, the apparent lack of connection between the various epistemes. The structure of inclusion and exclusion, bound up with Western science by the action of philosophy, is in fact the place where they come together or diverge. It thus grants unity to the succession of epistemes.

6. Non-Science

Let us look back again at the partitioned box that underlies all philosophies, and that each philosophy is required to "fill up." Once the authentic philosophical work of demarcation has been completed, various sciences are rejected and cast out, like the *mauvaises doctrines* eliminated by Descartes. Their free activity has been sentenced: a more and more compelling suspicion falls on them. A (−) sign of privation is superimposed on their concrete existence, a sign which attempts to eliminate precisely what this real presence desires, that is, the form of science. It denatures their presence, making them vacant and inactive. But it does not destroy: rather, it maintains this presence under the statutes of vacancy and inactivity, like a reference mark or an absence which enables a determined existence to make itself known.

The non-science designated by a given philosophical prosecution may strike us as incongruous. And in a certain sense it is. Astrology and scholasticism, banished by Cartesianism, come from quite different scientific traditions. And yet to the extent that both fall victim to this prosecution, they are closely linked. Non-science experiences something similar to what happened to "non-sense" in the seventeenth and eighteenth centuries: incongruous as it seems to us as an inclusive whole, as it did to the French revolutionaries, at the time it was perceived to be of one piece. What strikes us today as an amazing mélange of sodomites, madmen, libertines, prostitutes, atheists, and failed suicides can be viewed as a coherent whole only from the perspective of that period. It is precisely this *perspective* that should be analyzed if we are to disentangle the givens that make it possible. The same could be said about what any philosophy holds to be non-science. Certainly it is picturesque to lump together under the name of "metaphysics" such disparate creations as the philosophies of Hegel, Bergson, Heidegger and the so-called moral and theological sciences—misnamed, in Carnap's opinion. Since Carnap's prosecution, however, this grouping is a coherent whole.[18]

In order to perceive this coherence, however, a philosopher must *already have a definition* of what he has understood to be non-science or pseudo-science and be able to then account for and explain this potpourri. Non-science is therefore to some extent *outside* those discourses which are grouped together under this name. The sign given to them comes from without.

This accounts for the *phantom quality* of non-science. The grouping makes sense from the point of view and *within* that philosophy.

Today we use the name of *metaphysics* to indicate any form that transgresses our code of knowledge. We claim that metaphysical discourse is meaningless because its symbols are ambiguous, its statements inconsistent, or because it has no empirical foundation. We give the name of metaphysics today to all of those sciences to which we deny the very name of science. We have gone beyond metaphysics, we say, and we do not admit that we are safeguarding it and keeping it alive. Because we need metaphysics. Without it, how could we distribute the sign of scientificity or let it naturally adhere to certain fields of knowledge? We are only able to enact this ritual by virtue of the reference point represented by "metaphysics." Metaphysics is that invisible entity which allows others to become visible. It enables a certain sign or name to attach itself to certain discourses: it allows us to call these discourses *sciences*. Logical positivism and analytical philosophy in its cruder forms have not surpassed metaphysics. How can they, if they have invented it? These are the only philosophies which have brought an apparently disparate number of elements *together* under a single rubric which they of course had to have defined beforehand. They have created metaphysics in the same way that Fichte created dogmatism and Plato created sophistry. They have created the *modality* of non-science, the equivalent of the lineage of Terror in other modalities.

Logical positivism and its offspring keep metaphysics alive for one reason: because it is inseparable from the problems they attack. It is that "remote interior" which they both inhibit and elicit in their denunciation. Without realizing it, these watchdogs of knowledge, obsessed with metaphysics, are the guardians of metaphysics by virtue of their very obsession. The reason is obvious: What would happen if, in the long run, metaphysics was abolished? It would no longer be possible to demarcate in a positivist *manner*. The ritual process of demarcating could no longer be undertaken. Logical positivism and its offspring would disappear. If it had no progeny in the world of Terror, philosophy would fade away and "scientific knowledge" would vanish forever.

This is why the metaphysical genus must be *preserved*. Because if it vanished, who could come to grips even at a distance with the very philosophy that creates metaphysics? Metaphysics must be kept alive, even if it is excluded. Without it Neopositivism would suddenly cease to exist.

These observations enable us to explain the amusing relationship between those who accuse others of being metaphysical for Neopositivist or "analytical" reasons and the reactions of those who are thus singled out. Together both sides do a pretty dance of charge and countercharge which ensures that their dialogue, at a distance, stays alive. Because at bottom they understand each other. They are sustained and directed by the same structure. Essentially, they are actors in the same tragicomedy.

The "analytical" philosopher is thus arrogant and vain: not only has he not surpassed metaphysics, he cannot go beyond and destroy it without surpassing and destroying himself. He has done his best to keep it alive, if only in the realm of absence. The metaphysician's tears are likewise in vain: so-called "analytical" philosophy does not impinge on him at all. On the contrary, it grants him that domain of *exclusion* characterized by the time-honored, ambiguous prestige of what has been considered sacred, from shamanism and leprosy in the Middle Ages to metaphysics in the present. . . .

7. Philosophy's "Experimentum Crucis"

In chapter 3 of this essay we hinted at the distance that separates the methods used by Parmenides and Plato to establish a set of philosophical rules. While Parmenides does no more than simply and purely to enunciate a code, Plato *becomes aware* of the great difficulty involved in this undertaking. For this reason we differentiated between philosophical problems in an unconscious state (Parmenides) and what we might call self-conscious or *reflective* philosophical problems (Plato). In the pages that follow we will attempt to analyze more fully the totality of operations which explain the change from unconsciousness to consciousness. This will allow us to define *two general kinds of philosophical reflection* and to show that they recur throughout the "history" of philosophy.

Parmenides in effect does no more than enunciate a code, but
he does say that the code was given to him, that he received it from
the goddess. Whatever other meanings this may have, it helps us
to understand the extent to which the code is an unarguable "dic-
tate" which does not quite constitute a problem. We find something
similar in Descartes' *Regulae ad Directionem Ingenii,* where a set of
rules is announced which insures the "circulation," so to speak, and
progress of science. In Fichte's introductions to his *Science of Knowledge* we likewise find the pure and simple promulgation of a code
with which we can distinguish between a "basic science" ("marked"),
a science beginning with the Self's reflection on itself, and a science
which mistakes the ground for the grounded (the pseudoscience
Fichte calls "dogmatism"). In all three cases we are dealing with a
discourse which lays a set of rules abruptly on the table and distributes the "signs" corresponding to the sciences it takes into
consideration.

Let us now examine three discourses directly related to the three
we have mentioned while showing more sophisticated operating
procedures. We can verify how this procedure results in more
complex and sophisticated codes if we compare Parmenides' poem
to the Platonic dialogues, Descartes' *Regulae* to his own *Meditations,*
or Fichte's introductions to Hegel's *Phenomenology of Mind.* We can
say that in the latter works there is a (relative) growth of awareness
about what philosophical problems are, while in the former works
these problems *break into* the discourse without thereby creating
any consciousness. The diagram in figure 2.3 presents, in a provisional and "illustrative" sense, the typology of philosophies. Here
the use of the same letters indicates the material relationships between the philosophies, that is, the existence of the same *modality*
in the problems: a–a', b–b', c–c'.

Starting from a number of contemporary classifications of a historical nature, we can provisionally establish the categories in figure
2.4. Here the vertical order indicates *syntagmatic* relationships,
from our point of view, and the horizontal order represents *paradigmatic* relationships.

Figure 2.3

1. Naive discourse (no consciousness of the problems)
   a. Parmenides' poem
   b. Descartes' regulae
   c. Fichte's introductions
2. Sophisticated discourse (relative consciousness of problems)
   a'. Plato's dialogues
   b'. Descartes' meditations
   c'. Hegel's phenomenology

In the following pages we will try to isolate and define the "paradigm" underlying "sophisticated" discourse, which manifests itself in a series of recurring operations.

Let us take Plato's *Theaetetus* as a "referential" starting point. As Cornford has clearly demonstrated, this dialogue is really of a piece with the *Sophist*.[19] Together the two compose something like Plato's theory of knowledge. The issue at hand in the *Theaetetus* is the problem of knowledge, but only at the end of the *Sophist*, after a tortuous and so to speak dramatic analysis, is a way found to resolve the problem. The beginning of the *Theaetetus* gives us a clear idea of the distance that separates the dialogue from Parmenides' poem. Instead of framing the problem as an *answer* (that is, instead of actually stating the *problem*), Plato *asks* what knowledge is, through Socrates. This implies that, at least in the methodological

Figure 2.4

	Greek Philosophy	Rationalist Philosophy	German Idealism
Naive discourse	a	b	c
Sophisticated discourse	a'	b'	c'

sense, *we don't yet know what knowledge is* and that our ignorance is what we should examine with attention.

In this sense the question about what knowledge is, Socrates' *ti episteme*, implies that the object of the inquiry *has already been placed at some distance.* It also means that we are already conscious of the difficulty and the problematic nature of the question. What is more, this distance also indicates a (relative) *non-commitment* and *neutrality* with regard to the problem at hand. It is precisely this point which enables us, in the paradigmatic realm, to assimilate the Platonic dialogues to the *Meditations* and the *Phenomenology of Mind.* This distance means in effect that the issue of knowledge is raised and questioned, at least provisionally or in terms of "method." The philosopher assumes a position of independence from the object of the inquiry, which is defined differently in every case:

  a'. Socratic ignorance
  b'. Cartesian doubt
  c'. Hegelian doubt, skepticism, and despair

The *first act* of what we might call the *experimentum crucis* that philosophy undertakes with regard to knowledge is to invest this same triad of ignorance, doubt, and skepticism with importance. *Science* becomes effectively *relativized* and *denatured.* Science appears to the philosopher, in his neutrality, to be a *neutral* term receiving no *positive connotation.* The philosopher has done nothing less than provisionally or methodically withdraw all $(+)$ and $(-)$ *signs* from knowledge. But from which kind of knowledge? From what we might call *un-proven* knowledge.

This consequence is stated differently by different philosophies:

Socrates reduces knowledge to "opinion" ("they *think* they know but they do not Know," the capital K being the "plus" sign).
Descartes throws the whole of received knowledge into *doubt.*
Hegel teaches naive consciousness that it merely *believes* it knows.

Nevertheless, an *agent* is required to put this scheme of disillusionment in place. Now, the appearance of this agent presupposes a *second operation*:

The philosopher in effect acts the dramatic role of the *enemy of science*. In this capacity, he yields the floor to those shadowy discourses banished by naive prosecution from the realm of knowledge. He gives them the logos so that, armed with it, they can do battle against knowledge (naive logos). It enables them to fulfil their role as *anti*-logos, putting knowledge *to the test,* besieging it from all sides. For one instant the philosopher identifies with the shadows. This is the sense in which Plato unleashes sophistry, endowing it with speech with which to *express itself* in his dialogues. We see Socrates himself acting as if he were just another sophist practicing the cathartic version of the art defined by Plato which makes a failure of the man who believes himself knowledgeable while in fact receiving no new knowledge at all, except the knowledge of his own ignorance. The minor Socratic dialogues, all of which end in "failure," so to speak, beautifully embody this second aspect of the philosophical "experiment."

Similarly Descartes conjures the shades of the world of Terror and for an instant lets them vocally develop his doubt. First the madman arrives to besiege "sane" Reason. Later, man the dreamer relativizes this "wide-awake lucidity." Finally, the lying God turns the whole of Reason into a field of inquiry, including the consecrated disciplines like mathematics, the very method *naively* proposed by the young Descartes (the *regulae*). . . . The totality of Reason and "human discernment" becomes problematic with the dangerous knowledge of the lying God, that summary and compendium of the world of shadows. Descartes identifies, for an instant, with this terrible and enigmatic figure in order to put science to its hardest test.

Hegel does the same. With awe-inspiring lucidity he defines the Phenomenology of Mind as the path which leads to absolute Knowledge. It is a path of doubt and despair, the bitter cup and Calvary of the mind. He also defines the effort required to arrive at Knowledge as a "negative procedure." In this work Hegel identifies with the mammoth shadow of reflection, which works its corrosive power on every blossoming of human thought. Reflection reduces every one of the apparent forms of knowledge created by consciousness to the status of opinions: the result is the summa of errors that makes up the *Phenomenology*. Defined as consciousness's *experiment* on itself, this work is the most brilliant example of what we have defined as the first and second operations of the philosophical "experiment." As we shall soon see, it is also the perfect illustration of the third and final operation, which in the end is the decisive phase.

As a result of this operation science and non-science change roles. For an instant the shadows merge with the *logos* in order to sabotage knowledge, making it doubtful, disillusioning it. Non-science therefore *fulfills* a specific function: it withdraws the (+) sign from science when it is still naive, before it has proven its *mettle*.

There is no preventing this transformation:

$$\text{Non-science} \;\rightarrow\; \text{Science}_2 \;//$$
$$\text{Science}_1 \;\rightarrow\; \text{Non-science}$$

If we did not go beyond the result of the second transformation, we *would not have advanced at all*: we would only have inverted the roles. If that were the case the *new knowledge* resulting from the transformation (Science$_2$) would still have to be *tested*. There is no substantial difference between Science$_1$ and Science$_2$ on the "paradigmatic" level: both are forms of *naive knowledge*. The new knowledge which has appeared is not in a *tested* state. The experiment is therefore not over.

It is therefore necessary to follow the trajectory of ignorance, doubt, and despair beyond this petty accomplishment. A *third operation* corresponding to the acceleration of this trajectory must be added.

With this in mind let us repeat the operation, only in reverse:

$$\text{Non-science} \;\rightarrow\; \text{Science}_1 \;//$$
$$\text{Science}_2 \;\rightarrow\; \text{Non-science}$$

We hereby return to our point of departure, except that:

$$\text{Non-science} \;\rightarrow\; \text{Science}'_1 \;//$$
$$\text{Science}_2 \;\rightarrow\; \text{Non-science}'$$

where the ' sign indicates a difference which must be identified in relationship to the absence of a sign.

The third operation in effect carries on the trajectory of ignorance, doubt, and despair. The result of this prosecution presents three possibilities:

a. that it is nothing more than a return to the point of departure;

b. that one take the entire process into account and note "non-science's" effect on both Science$_1$ and Science$_2$.

c. that one note a special difference (') once the operation has been completed, a difference affecting Science$_1$.

The second alternative rules out the first, as it implies the clear recognition that both Science$_1$ and Science$_2$ have been affected by non-science, simultaneously neutralized and suppressed. In terms of Cartesian discourse, this means that doubt turns on itself: it both doubts itself and carries through with the operation on its own. Affected by non-science, doubt disappears, along with Socratic ignorance and Hegelian reflection. *This, the first alternative, leads to skepticism.*

But this second alternative also means a break in the "trajectory," because there is another possibility: that Socratic ignorance in the end reveals Knowledge of another sign written ('), like Cartesian doubt and Hegelian consciousness.

This is because, as the skeptic claims, doubt clearly dispels doubt when it *knows* that it doubts *without, on the other hand, dispelling this very knowledge*. Knowledge is not dispelled in the instant that doubt reflects on itself, far from it: it is this reflection, this Knowledge (') which has dispelled doubt. This kind of knowledge *leaves no room for doubt*. It is a certain knowledge: the Platonic episteme, Cartesian "discernment," Hegel's absolute knowledge. This Knowledge has been discovered within the trajectory. The very trajectory of Socratic ignorance has finally generated the knowledge: *I know that I know nothing.* This is the key to Socrates' superiority over the other *sophoi*, as the Oracle proclaimed. Socrates' knowledge *is already marked by another sign.* It implies the transformation:

$$S \rightarrow S'$$

The first tenet of Cartesianism does the same. It was necessary to discover the evidence of the Cogito in the very act of doubting, in that instant when doubt reflects on itself and *knows* that it has doubted. This is the one knowledge it could not doubt, obvious and certain as it is. In doubt it has found the certainty of a thought which can no longer doubt itself. And this "self-evident" idea belongs to a different realm in relation to the tenets of naive science. We are therefore observing the same transformation at work.

Virtually the same thing happens in the *Phenomenology of Mind.* It turns out, in the long run, that the "anti-logos" that constitutes the act of *reflection* becomes conscious of itself—of its own "negative procedure"—and considers itself the absolute knowledge. This knowledge is the despairing process of constant refutation and dissolution, a knowledge born of the "end of the road" where everyone *remembers* everyone else along with each and every one of the elements conserved or rejected. The negative procedure is revealed to Consciousness in the end as the activity of the Mind-in-and-for-itself. We observe the same transformation again.

We can already speculate as to what this transformation *means*: it marks the passage from a Science from which the sign that was attached to it (S$_1$) has been provisionally or methodically withdrawn to a Science that finally, justifiably, acquires a *sign* (S$'_1$). This (') sign is none other than the (+) sign that characterizes *marked* Knowledge. Once this marked Science is secured, we can also definitively withdraw the mark of Science from those discourses vying for the status of non-science which were aligned with naive knowledge before the experiment. It is now possible in effect to *demarcate* the Knowledge that Socrates invested with sophistic pseudoscience—the kind of science that lends itself to being developed into dialectical philosophy, the task accomplished by Plato in the *Sophist*—with the (−) sign that justly corresponds to it. The same holds true for Cartesian "discernment": once the evidence of the Cogito has been obtained there is a standard for evaluating the obvious or purportedly self-evident nature of philosophical statements. The (+) and (−) signs can then be assigned according to an "experimental" criterion, so to speak. The same is true in regard to Hegel's absolute knowledge, which is now, in Hegel's estimation, its own measuring stick: it can be used to judge all of those opinions which boast of being Science but which in reality are but stages in the development of Science.

At the end of the third stage we therefore witness the following transformation:

$$\text{Science}_1 \;\rightarrow\; \text{Science}'_1 \;\;//\;\; \text{Non-science} \;\rightarrow\; \text{Non-science}'$$

This is the same as:

$$\text{(Neutral) Science} \;\rightarrow\; (+)\,\text{Science} \;\;//$$
$$\text{(Neutral) Non-science} \;\rightarrow\; (-)\,\text{Non-science}$$

With this, philosophy has reached its *objective*: to solve the problem of demarcation, to sunder science from non-science and assign to each its proper sign.

8. Functions of the Split

In any case, both naive and sophisticated philosophies carry out the same activity: they split the totality of knowledge into the two zones of marked and unmarked knowledge. But what does this accomplish, what positive function does this division serve? What is the *positive* dimension of forbidding that certain roads be taken?

What, in other words, is the positive result of instituting a system of prohibitions and taboos in the heart of human knowing? What is accomplished by imposing these restrictions?

We will easily find the answer to these questions if we look at philosophy as a cultural artifact, that is, as an object that can be studied through the science of culture, through "ethnology." This entire essay is tacitly directed toward reinstituting what goes by the name of *metaphilosophy,* that is, philosophical inquiry within the field of ethnology or the science of culture.

From this point of view we will be able successfully to *extrapolate* a number of models which have facilitated the study of cultural structures in the area investigated by this essay.

As we have already seen, beginning with Parmenides philosophy takes on the form of a discourse which more than anything else *forbids* certain lines of inquiry. In order correctly to understand the positive counterpart to this prohibition we will examine a few rules operative in other areas of culture which are first and foremost prohibitions.

In the first essay we mentioned possible connections between "philosophical taboos" and the "incest taboo." We will now attempt to turn this somewhat frivolous remark into a properly grounded reflection. The principal object of study will be the incest taboo, a universal cultural rule.

In reality, this prohibition is nothing more than the "flip side" of a *prescription*. The positive counterpart to the incest taboo is indeed the *law of exogamy*. If we examine it in this way, we finally understand the *positive* function of the prohibition. When various *naturally* feasible types of matrimony are eliminated, the group is forced to look for women *outside* the family unit, in some *other* group. When men can no longer marry their sisters the masculine *ego* must search for women in another group and then *exchange his sisters* for these other women. The incest taboo effectively facilitates the change from the natural variety of relationships—kinship—to the social and cultural relationship of alliance through marriage. It makes men *donneurs* and *prenneurs*, and women become mercantile *goods* which make possible and sustain the alliance of one group with another. The law of exogamy enables both groups to work out a stable relationship based on the principle of reciprocity: it makes it possible for women to *circulate* between these groups. Given these premises, *different structures* (limited exchanges, general exchanges) come about. These structures are different ways of solving the problem of circulating women within the constraints of the rules of exogamy and the principles of reciprocity and alliance.[20]

Without pushing the analogy too far, we will attempt to use this model to solve the problem posed in this and the following chapters, namely, the problem of the positive function of the prohibition first enunciated by Parmenides.

As in the case of incest, the prohibition against traveling certain roads forces knowledge to renounce part of itself. In this way, however, it manages somehow to avoid *confusion*: it avoids the Babel of sciences in which different and contradictory inquiries are simultaneously held to be valid. It thereby avoids the promiscuity that characterizes all pre-philosophical knowledge.

Cartesian philosophy, for example, obliges "discernment" to forego inquiries like scholastic theology and astrology. By so doing it accomplishes two things: it limits a given science like physics or medicine to an exchange with related sciences like mathematics, insuring that the advances and discoveries of the different sciences circulate among them all. Philosophy thus gives the "green light" to certain sciences so that they can exchange their methods and achievements, and it enables new disciplines to obtain membership in the existing *scientific community* by following its *rules* (→), by making a contract with it. As in the case of kinship, there are a number of different modalities within the set of rules for the simple reason that all of them are trying to solve the same basic, operational problem: to insure the survival of a community which is subject to rules and to insure the free circulation of their *goods* ("knowing"). The fundamental accomplishment of this limiting of communication, the positive dimension applied to the whole of knowledge, is therefore that it establishes a community of disciplines and creates communication between the various members, achieving an interdisciplinary relationship and the use of a *common language*. This is why each philosophy brings a fresh approach to a number of intrinsic problems, specifically the problem of the *unity of science* and the problem of a unified language. In a structuralist sense we might say that these problems depend on the basic, universal problem of all philosophy (without which philosophy does not exist): the problem of demarcation. After this, however, they are the most basic and universal problems. In this way the problem of the "unity of science" enjoys the status of a "perennial concern," and we see it raised expressly in Plato and Descartes, Fichte and logical positivism, etc.

The split of knowledge into two areas thus allows the formation of an (inclusive) community whose subgroups and corresponding members can at last communicate with each other and exchange "goods." The sine qua non of this circulation of knowledge is, in this sense, a form of *intersubjectivity* (usually called "objectivity") insured by a set of norms. This intersubjectivity takes shape in a common, "unified" language which makes possible an exchange of "messages." The "grammatical" rules of this language make possible the flawless reception of the message, which in turn is insured by the codified community of sender and receiver. Community, the consciousness of community, intersubjectivity, the possibility of exchange and communication: these, then, are the positive outgrowths of the split at the heart of knowledge.

Its negative dimension is the loss of a broader community in which there are no restrictions or exclusions, in which what is "included" and what is "excluded"—the *Self* and the *Other*—still speak to each other, even at the risk of creating mayhem and disorder or a touch of anarchy—a broader community in which knowledge has not yet suffered the split that happens at the precise moment when philosophy comes into its own.

We can therefore say that the sundering of knowledge—philosophy—carries on the *cultural task* initiated by the incest taboo and the law of exogamy. The absolute universality of these phenomena suggests the hypothesis that it is an autonomous (cultural) order which adds itself to nature. The prohibition in effect *intervenes* in the natural order when it forbids certain naturally feasible "exchanges." But far from being irrational and arbitrary this intervention is only "arbitrary" in relationship to the biological factor: it follows a different kind of criteria, criteria of social and cultural rationality. The law of exogamy effectively substitutes the social ties of alliance for the natural ties of kinship. Similarly, the sundering of knowledge substitutes an interrupted and preplanned progress, so to speak, for the (relatively) spontaneous progress of knowledge. Philosophy means, then, that the cultural stigma attached to the prohibition of incest in the social realm suddenly appears in the heart of the totality of human knowledge.

9. Knowing and "Scientific Knowledge"

Before Parmenides and in the magical or mythical thinking that we associate with supposedly primitive cultures we find no trace of problems like those hinted at in Parmenides' poem and consciously developed in Plato's *Theaetetus*. The question *ti episteme* and all of the activities that come with it seem to be a genuinely Greek reflection. These problems do not appear in other cultures, nor of course do their consequences in the realm of knowledge, namely, the appearance of the structure of inclusion and exclusion at the core of knowing.

This is an important point to stress, as it does away with a lot of meaningless talk about the meaning of the evolution from so-called "mythical thought" to "philosophical talk." Philosophy does not represent, as has so often been stated, the first manifestation of "abstract" thought liberated from the trappings of imagery. Nor is it the culmination of human consciousness or its reduction to a single concept which summarizes the entire universe, a concept like "being," for instance, as explained by Parmenides. Ever since Mauss's work we have known that the so-called primitive peoples possess categories of similar subtlety and scope, like the notion of "manna."[21] In addition, a lexeme in any language implies a choice or "abstraction," if you will, from the inchoate mass of sensory data collected without a conscious criterion, without a basis (or "motivation") in things themselves. Subtlety and cleverness must not be measured so much by the ability to create concepts like "beings," which are as broad as they are hollow, as by the ability to develop subtle distinctions in the very heart of what seems to be most homogeneous, such as the rich botanical and zoological lexicons of many peoples thought to be primitive. Philosophy, then, is not the evolution from Myth to Logos or anything like it. It means rather that the conditions have been set in which "free" science can become knowledge sundered from non-science.

In this sense the prohibition against following certain lines of inquiry fulfills a function similar to that of the incest taboo. The latter is in effect the precondition of or a priori to the evolution from natural relationships (kinship) to sociocultural relationships (alliance). Similarly, to the extent that philosophy gives the "red light" to certain areas of knowledge, it is the *condition of possibility* of the evolution from a "free" Knowledge (limited only by norms implicit to itself) to a different realm: it is the condition of possibility of a new "scientific knowledge" sundered from non-science.

Incest taboo:
  natural relationships   →   social relationships

Philosophy:
  free knowledge   →   scientific knowledge (and non-science)

This is an important point, and it is surprising that it has not been made before, because it explains at one and the same time:

  a. the function of philosophy with regard to knowledge;
  b. the unique characteristics of a kind of knowledge which continually elicits philosophical reflection, as if it were a strange humor. This is, in as few words as possible, what makes *Western science* what it is in relationship to other "kinds of knowledge." It is the *split* between two general kinds of knowledge;
  c. various relationships between cultural structures—in this instance, between the structures of kinship and the structures of knowledge.

In reference to ethnology and its precarious ways of explaining the prohibition against incest, Lévi-Strauss asks: "how could rules be analyzed and interpreted if ethnology should confess its help-lessness before the one preeminent and universal rule which assures culture's hold over nature?"²² Culture, which is the "universe of laws," can only be understood if this universal Law, erected as a prohibition in all societies, can be investigated. Only in this way can culture become the autonomous domain of a discipline (ethnology or anthropology).

By comparison with the incest taboo, the "prohibition against traveling certain roads" has a less universal, more specific nature. The comparison between the two suggested by point (c) above should therefore be made cautiously. Simply because they have the same value does not mean that they are comparable. The relationship between them is actually based on the fact that one of them (philosophy) presupposes the other (incest taboo). Their relationship is therefore one of dependency. We might go so far as to say: philosophy *is* the incest taboo at work in the heart of human knowledge. The taboo is in effect the a priori of human culture and society. It is refracted in one way or another in the various relatively autonomous spheres of the realm which it alone enables to flourish as a system. Its inflection in the domain of knowledge is philosophy.

Once these approximations have been made, we can then ask the same question in regard to a much more limited domain: How can we investigate or analyze the history of Western philosophy and science without having first given a valid explanation of that Law (taboo) which permeates all of Western science, setting it apart from the science of other cultures?

10. The Structure of "Science/Non-Science"

Throughout this essay we have referred to the *structure* of science and non-science. We should explain why we call this relationship a "structure." The reader may have wondered if our constant use of this term constitutes an unconfessed concession to a trend. I do not rule this out altogether. Far worse and more dangerous than trendiness, I think, is the "enlightened" approach of systematically rejecting all trends. This is not the place to analyze the philosophy of boredom that such an approach presupposes, although I intend to do so some day. But as far as the matter at hand is concerned, the use of this term is justified because "structure" denotes that all of the elements that make up a structure are interrelated in such a way that altering one implies modifying the *value* of all the others.

With this in mind it will help to go back to figure 2.2. Both constant and variable terms are included in it. The three compartments (right, left, and center) and the signs ($+$, $-$, and $\pm$) are always the same, while the "contents" change according to changes in the rules or criteria of demarcation. One could actually speak of a constant (formal) structure and different *ways* in which the contents are structured.

The structural nature of the formal scheme presents no problems, since none of its constituent elements can appear without the others: the presence of one implies the presence of all the others. Finally, the substitution of one element by an element from outside the structure invalidates the entire configuration. Regarding the "structural" nature of the contents, we must make something clear: on the one hand, the presence of any single element is linked to the presence of a given kind of rules. An analysis of the conceivable orders of succession of these rules is beyond the scope of this essay, although it will be undertaken in the following essay. On the other hand, however, it is possible to discover a *formal succession of contents,* so to speak, with the following implications: marked and unmarked contents are linked together in such a way that any change in any one of the contents—their substitution by another element or the presence of an element not belonging to the group in any of the compartments—necessarily creates a change in the *kind* of relationship between science and non-science. In the previous essay we suggested a relationship of this kind when we examined Fichte's enunciation of the "science/non-science" dichotomy in terms of a dichotomy between "idealism" and "dogmatism."

Each of these elements implied a "structural" relationship with the other. This relationship enables us to formulate the hypothesis that all philosophies create, next to the established and "marked" system, an inhibited system which, because it is "denounced," is also that philosophy's *shadow*. Between idealism and dogmatism we therefore see such a strict interrelationship that any change in any of the constituent elements has an immediate repercussion in the other elements. This is why we cannot substitute "dogmatism" for any other form of "non-science" (sophistry or metaphysics, for example) without bringing about an ipso facto modification of the semantic value of the term "subjective idealism."

On the other hand, we should forestall a possible misunderstanding: when we speak of "non-science" we are not referring to "something which is not" this or that kind of knowing. Non-science is not knowledge "out of season" but rather the *inner transcendence* of knowledge, its *shadow*. As soon as philosophy makes its entrance there is no "knowledge" without this accompanying "twin," and this "other" is always *perfectly well-defined*. It has its own fixed boundaries and limits: it is, in a word, established. What is "excluded" is not simply the exterior, absolute darkness, but rather, as Althusser has said, "the inner darkness of exclusion."[23] Our confusion and misunderstanding comes from always clinging to a given prosecution. We tend to extrapolate concrete examples of non-science (or "nonsense") as universal or natural entities. Philosophies are always falling victim to this ideological (or if you prefer, "ethnocentric") mirage in respect to what they stipulate as instances of both "non-science" and "science." They therefore believe that they have solved the problem of demarcation, and all the attendant problems, "once and for all."

In any case, philosophies always tend to confuse their actual, specific problems with the "form" these problems take. They believe that they have *finally* solved the problem of demarcation and thereby set science off in the right direction. When they express themselves in terms of "science" and "metaphysics," for example, they believe that both terms correspond exactly to the "compartmentalized square," without taking notice of the fertile, age-old

lineage that has paraded through the same "compartments." This
kind of mirage in part explains the possible confusion between
"general non-science" and what we understand non-science to be
here: the well-defined, clearly marked, concrete set of discourses
which every philosophical prosecution brands with the negative
sign, the entity defined by every philosophy in a different and
elemental *way* as sophistry, dogmatism, metaphysics, etc.

Our discovery of a *structure* of science and non-science at the
heart of Western science also enables us to avoid the pitfalls of an
"archeology of knowledge" that cannot explain the "breaks" that
have occurred in "Western thought" from the Renaissance to the
present. From *The Order of Things* one gathers that the various
"epistemes" neither communicate among themselves nor share anything in common. Eighteenth-century "natural history," so carefully
analyzed by Foucault, appears to provide a model for this surprising
inquiry, which might be called "continuity and catastrophe."[24] This
is why some critics have concluded that, more than an archaeology,
what is here in question is a "geology," because a cataclysm me-
diates between all of the "epistemes" creating an "epistemological
field" completely unrelated to what went before.[25] Foucault himself
admits that these "breaks" remain "enigmatic." There is no explanation for them—what is more, there can be no explanation for
them: they are a constant enigma confronting the human reason.
In order to understand them reason would have to establish itself
outside its own episteme, and this is impossible. The episteme is
tyrant and terrorist. It binds us to its unyielding conditions, and
we can think and feel from its viewpoint alone.

Like Piaget, Foucault therefore eventually concludes that reason
transforms itself unreasonably.[26] In a way, he subscribes to the
highly debatable Saussurian notion of "diachrony," which states
that the change from one "synchrony" to another cannot be explained by any law or rule. Foucault thus refuses to study the change
from one episteme to the next on the grounds that the phenomenon
is "mysterious."

The criticism we are making is simply that one should not unconditionally accept this notion and the "philosophy of history" underlying it. But by doing just that Foucault is closing off a direction of study which he himself so masterfully mapped out. His identification of the various epistemes is in fact an important step, a "stage" of inquiry similar to what Lévi-Strauss defines as the "analysis of differences." Foucault reveals schisms and gaps in the mythical continuity or evolution of the sciences. But Lévi-Strauss also stresses that the inquiry cannot stop at this stage but must rather go on to study the whole all over again, this time from the vantage point of its incongruities, explaining the latter by recourse to the former. In this way we can discover the rule that explains the "transformations."[27]

Our hypothesis that there is a structure which simultaneously unites philosophical discourse, clarifies its relationship to knowledge, and gives unity to "Western science," is a step in this direction. On a deeper, more ancient and universal level than Foucault's "episteme" we find a structure that is visible in *all* "epistemes" and in Western science in general.

This study is nevertheless nothing more than that: a step forward. It does not come close to defining standards which cannot yet be foreseen. The structure we are presenting is still *schematic* and *static*. It in no way explains the rule which determines whether a content will be included or excluded.

Our inquiry is not therefore "transformational," even though in the following essay we will attempt to abstract an order from the contents we have been discussing. In order to do this we will adopt a different model.

We are aware of the limitations of our approach, but we believe that our hypothesis enables us to take the first step toward overcoming the "Saussurianism" implicit in the works of Foucault.[28]

11. Western Culture

In the course of this essay we have established two aspects of the function of philosophy: (1) Philosophy is a *supplementary cod-*

ification of knowledge; (2) Philosophy allows the structure of inclusion and exclusion to make its presence felt in the sciences. Before drawing a conclusion we should speak of the *cultural mark* and the *overall structure* that explain both of these aspects. Finally, we shall suggest a tentative interpretation of the *meaning* of this structure.

Is there, in effect, any culture which shows a tendency to *supercodify* in *different realms*? Can we find a culture which manifests the inclusion/exclusion structure in *different domains*?

In answering the first question we will do well to consult the work of that great pioneer in the *ethnology of Western culture,* Friedrich Nietzsche. In answering the second, we must take into account Michel Foucault's *Madness and Civilization,* perhaps the most lucid work in the area first described by Nietzsche.

We will make no attempt, in this essay at least, to analyze Nietzsche's vast work. We will be content to mention a few aspects of his theory of Western culture which will enable us to understand the first function of philosophy as stated immediately above.

For Nietzsche, philosophy is one of the "highest values" of Western culture, along with religion and ethics.

Nietzsche sees philosophy as something more than a simple "pattern" of behavior (that is, more than a *motivating* or *guiding* force behind behavior). A "highest value" is a *reflection,* so to speak, on the simple patterns that determine human life and behavior, a reflection which tends to purify certain implicit behavioral norms, rendering them more complex and justifying them as well. The "highest values" *add* an *additional set of norms,* so to speak, to existing social and cultural norms. In this sense morality *sits astride* the norms that determine social and institutional life and customs, subjecting them, like the law, to a process of recodification.

Nietzsche's thesis is that Western culture tends to create this kind of "supreme value" added to the implicit rules of the entire culture. Like ethics, Western religion tends to subject (relatively) free religious experience to a strict *theological* codification which cramps and narrows that experience. Philosophy can be seen to repeat this same procedure in relation to science. The highest values thus constitute a "duplicate" or "second-rate" culture which stands at the furthest possible remove from natural, instinctive vitality. The Western experience in this sense is synonymous with an *excess* of culture at the expense of nature and life. This explains the unilateral character and the "nihilistic" tendency of Western culture (it embodies "Culture" at the expense of "natural, instinctive Vitality," the latter being, for Nietzsche, authentic reality):

Other societies: Nature   →   Culture$_1$
The West: Nature   →   Culture$_1$ →   Culture$_2$

where Culture$_2$ is the totality of "highest values."

Nietzsche's idea of Western culture is much more than pure theory: it is a provocative working hypothesis expressing a *general tendency* clearly visible in the West. The fact that some of these "highest values" have come about *previously* or *as well* in other cultures does not present an obstacle, as Nietzsche simply claims that they evolved spontaneously or almost spontaneously in the West alone, in this way achieving their ultimate perfection and subtlety.

In any case, it is a working hypothesis which enables us to understand exactly what makes or has made Western culture different from other cultures, once its validity has been ascertained. In one sense our essay is an attempt to show how we go about verifying one of the crucial aspects of Nietzsche's notion, namely, his conclusion that philosophy is one of the West's "highest values."

Nietzsche's hypothesis also helps us to understand what we might call the *systematic* nature of philosophy. This has not come about in just any culture: it has come about precisely in that culture which is characterized and made unique by its *doubling* of the norms that constitute cultures in general. To this extent philosophy puts into action Western culture's *intentions* in the area of knowledge.

Finally, this hypothesis suggests a number of *interdependent relationships* between the "highest values" created by the West. Western philosophy, ethics, and religion result from the establishment of this "secondary culture" (Culture₂) unique to the West. In this secondary culture the implicit norms of all cultures are duplicated in a supplementary set of norms.

The hypothesis ultimately allows us to articulate a number of other hypotheses useful in formulating a general theory of culture or ethnology. We pointed out above that philosophy *presupposes* a cultural realm subject to rules which are made possible by the universal Rule (of incest). Hence its *dependence* on the latter. While the incest rule laid the basis for culture in general, philosophy (and by extension the "highest values" of the West) laid the bases for a new cultural order (Culture₂), although restricted to the relatively autonomous realm of science (see figure 2.5).

Regarding the second function of philosophy, the introduction to *Madness and Civilization* enables us to assign the proper *mark* to this characteristically philosophical activity. Foucault here attempts to carry on Nietzsche's project by studying the *foundations* and *limitations* ("boundary situations") of Western culture. He is trying above all to articulate an "archeology of Western culture."[29]

Foucault identifies a number of "scissions" at the very *root* of Western culture: "culture in general" is split into "East and West"; social life is split into "reason" and "non-reason"; the life of the mind is split into "waking" and "dreaming" existence; the "ebullient

Figure 2.5

Incest:
nature →   culture₁
Philosophy: culture₁   (realm of science) →   culture₂
  ↕
Ethics: culture₁   (realm of mores) →   culture₂
  ↕
Religion
(Western):   culture₁   (realm of Religious
                           Activities) →   culture₂

life of desire" is split into "sexual normalcy" and "perversion." In an earlier work he breaks religious experience into the duality of the "sacred" and the "profane."[30] Finally, the life of the individual is divided between "infancy" and "maturity."

This might appear outlandish, but only on first impression. Foucault has actually chosen a very solid model upon which to elaborate his inventory.

His model is *Freudian.* In that he brought to light those areas which had traditionally been considered empty of meaning—infant sexuality, dreams, the deliria of "madmen," etc.—Freud was actually a pioneer researcher into the origins of Western culture. The very fact that these areas were left unstudied for so long is a sure indication that they are *inhibited* areas: the dangerous possibility of their coming to the fore was blocked by the ideological decision that they were "meaningless." In studying several types of insanity Freud discovered a series of mechanisms common to both the rantings of the "insane" and the symbolism of dreams. He explained these mechanisms as desires set free after having been profoundly repressed since earliest childhood. He went on to draw a general diagram of the human mind based on the primary mechanisms of the unconscious.

What Freud really discovered, however, were the unconscious mechanisms of "Western man." He extrapolated this brilliant insight on "Western culture" into the domain of general anthropology. Foucault attempts, in this respect, to reverse the road traveled by Freud: instead of extrapolating to the general realm of anthropology the mechanisms lodged in the unconscious minds of Europeans, he tries to observe the very birth of these mechanisms from a different, prior anthropological viewpoint. He asks: Under what conditions can the following phenomena come about—(1) insanity; (2) a dream life separate from waking existence; (3) the iron curtain of "forgetfulness" that separates childhood from adulthood; (4) the banishment of the "transcendent experience of the holy" to the realm of private, individual delirium; (5) the limitation of acts provoked by desire by restraints imposed by the most tyrannical of inhibitions. He attempts to analyze the conditions of possibility of each of these premises. Psychoanalysis may assume that they are givens, but they are in fact "givens" specifically and exclusively in Western culture alone.

Western culture in effect *conceives* of each of these realms as *dualities*. It tends to *retain* one of the terms while *expelling* the other. The West thus rejects dreams on the grounds that they are irrelevant, meaningless, and "absurd." It rejects the ebullient life of desire on the grounds that it is "deviant." It defines those who are socially ostracized as "insane" or "mad." It views transcendent experiences as "private delusions" (the same for mysticism), while at the same time making religion "profane." Finally, it conceives of adulthood as the total loss of childhood memories, as scission from childhood. It then doubles all of these scissions by adding a kind of *science* which considers one member of the pair as "rational" while the other is "irrational." Ontologically, this science is doubled by a distinction between "real" and "unreal."

In other cultures, however, there is scarcely any discernible difference between dream life and waking life. Rather, the former is a source of inspiration and motivation of events that take place in the latter.[31] Although "social exclusion" exists in so-called primitive societies it does not belong to the category of "insanity."[32] The condition of possibility of insanity has been the scission of Western society into two halves, one of them consisting of what is "included"—sanity, normalcy—and the other of what is "excluded"—madness, "insanity." The exclusion is also reinforced by *confinement* in asylums and institutions. Other cultures have not separated the realm of the sacred from that of the profane, as the West has done, in such a radical fashion. In most so-called primitive cultures it is virtually impossible, as Mauss eventually confesses, to tell the one from the other.[33] The West is also unique in the number of taboos it has attached to human desire in the interests of restraining it.

In all of these realms of human life we can see the other *design* of Western culture at work. A complement to what we have been discussing, it enables us to expand Nietzsche's idea of Western culture to include the *scission* of different sectors like society, psychology, sex, religion, and individual experience into pairs consisting of a *marked* and an unmarked component. *The structure of inclusion and exclusion*—or as Foucault would say, "the Self and the Other"—*is thus born in all of these realms* (see figure 2.6).

The list in figure 2.6 may seem incongruous, but it has a coherence, as we have seen, to be found in the Freudian model that inspires Foucault to "turn the tables," so to speak, on psychology by examining the roots of the model. In any event, the approach is provocative, judging from the partial but nevertheless extraordinary evidence of *Madness and Civilization*. Based on the scheme of opposing pairs, this work demonstrates, by exhaustive historical analysis, how the West has maintained the structure of inclusion and exclusion in the "social" realm ever since the Renaissance. It shows how "social rejects" have been first expelled from the community and then institutionalized. Called "mad" at first, these individuals are later labeled "crazy" or "mentally ill"—as they are today—thus making possible a "psychology of mental illness" that is supposedly "positivist," "objective," "empirical."

This "provisional diagram" at least allows us to state the following hypothesis: the *design* of Western culture—that is, what makes it different from other cultures—is, on the one hand, that it *doubles* cultural rules by adding additional codes to them and on the other hand that it *splits all realms of human existence into dualities* in a manner which complements the doubling of rules. In each duality or pair one member is accepted and the other rejected: the scission between what is "included" and what is "excluded," between the "Self" and the "Other," is recreated in each and every domain. Is

Figure 2.6

Realm	*Included*	*Excluded*
Society	Normalcy	Madness or "insanity"
Psychology	Waking life	Dreams
Sex	Normalcy	"Deviance"
Religion	Profane	Sacred
Individual life	Adulthood	Childhood

not the *structure of inclusion and exclusion* then the *overall structure* of Western society—that which underlies and so well explains both its history and its authentic creations?

In order to answer this question we should properly study each of these "domains," following Foucault's example in *Madness and Civilization*. The present essay is nothing more or less than an attempt to study this structure in the *domain of knowledge*. We therefore propose the following addition to the preceding diagram:

Realm	Included	Excluded
Knowledge	(+) Science	(−) Non-science

This is possible because philosophy is that "highest value" which enables us to complete this scission and the exclusion which follows from it.

With this our assertion that philosophy allows the structure of inclusion and exclusion to *emerge* in the sciences can be seen in all of its ramifications. This structure does not rule out science but rather constitutes the unconscious foundation, so to speak, of Western culture. Nevertheless, without philosophy this structure does not become *visible* in the relatively autonomous domain of science. We might say that with the appearance of philosophy the *overall structure* of Western culture emerges in the domain of knowledge, taking *specific shape* within given domains. Parodying Hegel, we might say that with philosophy the "universal abstract" which constitutes this structure becomes an "actual universe." *Universal* to the extent that it pervades the entire sphere of Western culture. *Concrete* to the extent that it is *refracted* in the relatively autonomous sphere of knowledge. *Philosophy allows the refraction of this structure in the domain of knowledge.*

Conclusion

At the beginning of this essay we asked what were the purpose and structure of philosophy and what was its characteristic set of problems. In answering these questions we found ourselves exploring nothing less than a structure which constantly recurs in "Western science." And yet we could not pause and put our inquiry to rest at that stage, as we found ourselves then investigating the roots of this science in the *overall structure of Western culture*. Fortunately, we were helped at that point by the provocative analyses of Nietzsche and Foucault. These enabled us properly to demarcate the conclusions of our analysis and to take the first steps toward a general interpretation of Western culture in relation to other cultures. Our intention of analyzing philosophy from an *ethnological* and *anthropological* point of view thus became fully meaningful.

Many loose ends have nevertheless come unraveled along the way. We may have made use of too many "daring" or uncautious conjectures, for example. We are fully aware of these risks, but they have been unavoidable: we ventured into a virgin forest where we had to cut makeshift paths at the risk of their leading "nowhere." We had to approach our subject—what is philosophy and what does it mean?—from a radically original perspective, because the question is as poorly understood as it is frequently asked. We were therefore obliged to set foot on hostile territory.

In conclusion: in outlining a "general theory of philosophy" we have been guided to a "general theory of Western science" and from there to a "general theory of Western culture" within the context of "culture in general" (i.e., ethnology). Are these perhaps not too many "theories" for such a short essay? Certainly. But we are not in the least alarmed by this profusion. After all, as Novalis said, theories are like nets: if you don't cast them, you don't catch anything.

3

Philosophy Without Man

INTRODUCTION

1. The Problem

One thing in any case is certain: man is neither the oldest nor the most constant problem that has been posed for human knowledge.[1]

Michel Foucault may well arrive at this conclusion after a 386-page voyage through time, beginning with the Renaissance and ending today. This exploration of the various "fields" in which the floral species of Western thought have bloomed culminates in a vision of a new field in which a number of the previously most valued plants will have withered and died. In the field of knowledge currently being seeded there may be no place for the species called "man," that unique crop of the so-called "social sciences." Foucault is equally powerless to prevent its extinction: he limits himself to betting on its disappearance.[2]

The proof is as simple as it is forceful. Our sciences are more and more clearly oriented in view of the irrefutable fact that we possess languages and systems of signs, values, and interaction. We

no longer answer as Nietzsche did the question "Who is speaking?"
with "Ecce homo." Like Mallarmé, we answer "Language is speaking." To the question "Who is at work here?" we no longer give
the humanist answer "Man is at work here." We answer quite
differently, saying that the social class, the group or the system is
at work here.[3]

"Man" therefore ceases to be a relevant "scientific concept" in
a theory of social change (Althusser). He can no longer have any
place in "Theory" (Althusser again) nor, generally speaking, in the
epistemological field in which burgeoning social sciences like psychoanalysis, ethnology, and linguistics take on the task of "dissolving man" (Lévi-Strauss), eviscerating the ancient, consecrated
attributes that used to clothe the figure of man and substituting
anonymous or unconscious systems for them. In this sense psychoanalysis subjects man to the "ultimate humiliation," robbing
him of his most coveted attribute: "self-consciousness." Since Saussure and Sapir linguists have affirmed the unconscious nature of
linguistic processes; the same is true of contemporary ethnology
since Boas. The "human individual," viewed as an empirical unit
or his collective hypostasis (that is, Man with a capital M), has
ceased to be the "irrefutable fact" that was the starting point of all
inquiries. The starting point is now "social relationships" (Marx)
and "social facts" (Durkheim) and language as a social institution
(Saussure), etc.[4]

Man, the human subject, is effaced, withers, and dies. The social
sciences are no longer "human." The economy of knowledge leaves
no room for man. The phenomenon can also be observed on other
levels. Since Marx, the agents of social change are classes, not
"men." The social classes have exclusive claim to "praxis," independently from what individual men think and desire. Desire and
thought—the double dimension of man considered by all humanistic philosophies since Kant to be the starting point of all
"works"—now become merely consequential. The "works" have
killed the "men," but not in Unamuno's sense of the work's revolt
against its author. The work is no longer answerable to any author:
it sustains itself within its own anonymity. Cultural works refer
back to cultural structures, social works to social structures. "Struc-

ture" with a capital S is the new deity created by our science every time it abandons "methodological" caution and objectifies its epistemological codes. Man's Divine Nature enters into a decline. "Radical theology," which finally found in MAN a way of filling the void and idleness created by the "death of God," faces the prospect of unemployment again. New, anonymous and impersonal Gods nevertheless appear on the horizon. The reign of the God of the "Self" succeeeds the reign of Man's Divine Nature. The "person," the "I" and the "thou" and the whole rather banal poetry of their relationships as intoned by all the more or less confessional phenomenologies, dialectics, and existentialisms give way to this "third party" who is not exactly a person. "Oneself" speaks, "Oneself" acts, "Onself" writes, one knows "Oneself": suddenly, the "Self" acquires the *inverse* attributes of the individual human being. It is neither individual nor is it conscious. The new, incipient philosophy is still defined negatively: it is philosophy without man, the philosophy of the death of man.[5]

In this essay we are of course taking note of all the commonplaces on which our reflection comfortably rests. Whether we like it or not, our reflection is implied in the debate and complicated by it. Is "man" still a "problem"? Does a philosophy of man, a philosophical anthropology, still have any meaning? Is it enough to speak of the "human sciences"? Can one be or continue being a "humanist" nowadays? Is there any sense in asking "What is man"? No sooner have we established the matter we wish to investigate than all of these questions start buzzing around our heads.

Should we present arguments for and against Foucault's bet on the extinction of man in the "field" of knowledge or in the social theories and theories of knowledge which, like Althusser's, refuse to incorporate the notion of mankind? Should we rather take up the opinions of humanists and antihumanists or brazenly bare our emotions "pour l'Homme" (Dufrenne) or in favor of Systems (Foucault)?[6]

This essay does not enter directly into this debate. It attempts to prove the validity or nonvalidity of a thesis regarding man's extinction in the "relatively autonomous" realm of philosophy. Our journey somewhat resembles Foucault's, except that instead of ex-

amining the middle ground between language and scientific theory—a more basic domain, to the extent that it constitutes an
"episteme"—or beginning with the foundations of the scientific
edifice, it starts out from the roof. It is not, therefore, "another"
archaeology of knowledge. It studies only certain characteristic
"philosophies" of Western culture including Plato, Descartes, Kant,
and what appears to be the dominant philosophy of the moment.
Philosophy has always been a reflection on knowledge. It is the
answer to Socrates' question, *ti episteme?* It is a secondary activity
with limited interest as an "archaeology" but great fascination as
a symptom. Philosophy is the thermometer of knowledge, and at
times it is most definitely out of whack.

Several texts—among them Plato's, Descartes', and Kant's—
form the basis of the essay. Several principles determine the criterion applied in dividing and arranging these texts.

First of all, we assume that all of these texts tackle the same
problem: the problem of knowledge. In all of them this problem
implies the following questions: Who is it who knows? What does
that person know? How is it that the knower knows that what is
"knowable" is in fact known? The pertinent terms of the problems
raised in these texts are: knower, known, condition of knowing.
Each text must in some way account for the categories implied by
each of these terms.

First and foremost, we find in each of these texts the "sine qua
non" of knowing, the "unconditioned condition" which carries with
it the key to knowledge and science. We will attempt to identify
this unconditioned condition, what Plato called the "anhypotheton," in each of the texts in question.

The texts will be arranged and divided according to the possible
dislocations that the unconditioned condition seems to bring about.
Each dislocation implies the creation of a different *epistemological
configuration*. We can portray these configurations according to
whether the unconditioned condition is "external" or "internal"
with respect to the knower and the known. They will also be
distinguishable by the degree to which they lean toward the knower
or the known.

Given these definitions, we can state the problem as follows: Is there any configuration in which "man" occupies not only a relevant place at the heart of the epistemological whole but also a commanding position as the "unconditioned condition" of knowledge and science? When does this configuration first appear and when does it disappear?

Furthermore, in which configuration do we find ourselves today? Does "man" have any *place* in this configuration? These questions constitute the plot of the following investigation, which attempts, hypothetically, to answer them.

2. The Model

The foregoing propositions clearly indicate the method we will use. The objective is to discover the various orientations of a structure built on the following constants: knower, known, unconditioned possibility of knowing. The second of these two terms is *mobile*: each of its *displacements* describes a different *configuration*. Before proceeding to study each of these displacements concretely, however, we will make an a priori model describing the ways in which this term may *possibly be channeled*.

To begin with, we are presented with an option. The unconditioned (a) may be *external* or *internal* to the knower/known pair. Secondly, it may *affect one* of the two terms or the *relationship* between the terms (see figure 3.1).

Figure 3.1

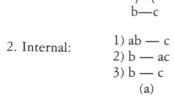

1. External:

$$\begin{array}{c} a \\ / \ \backslash \\ b \text{---} c \end{array}$$

2. Internal:

1) ab — c
2) b — ac
3) b — c

(a)

Figure 3.2

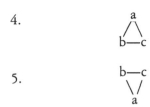

4.

5.

Now, we can resolve this "external" aspect by selecting one of two options: an exterior of "height" (4) or an exterior of "depth" (5). The former means that the "unconditioned" *transcends* b–c, while the latter means that it *lies beneath*, so to speak (see figure 3.2).

Once this has been assumed, we need only remember that each displacement of "a" alters the *value* of the remaining terms. With this model we can isolate five configurations, the second of which we will ignore for reasons explained in the conclusion.

We will follow a chronological order that can be stated as follows:

1. Kant
2. Historical Platonism (not taken into account)
3. Descartes
4. Platonic philosophy
5. Present-day philosophy

PART I: PROMOTION

1. The Epistemological Triangle (*Republic* 507a–509c)

I

It would appear that genuine knowledge comes about when the soul ceases wandering within the narrow sphere of material bodies, detaches itself from sense perceptions and liberates a kind of intelligence which looks to the unchanging aspect of things (*eidos*). Genuine knowledge, then, requires an intelligence that is not tied to sense perceptions. It also requires an intelligible world that can be told apart from the material world. The "eye of the soul" and "ideas" will be the preconditions of knowledge. Following clues that can be detected in the shadows of the material world—like reflections or copies of another world—the soul awakes from its dull slumber. Beauty continues to exist in "beautiful things," and the trace of permanent characteristics can be found in the uniqueness and constant changefulness of worldly things. The soul, free at last from the body and its changeful senses, delivered from its chains, puts its intellectual faculties to work, turning its gaze toward objects full of light. It is bathed in the light that streams from those objects.

Socrates, however, explains the process in a different way. The light received by the soul when it is freed from the changeful senses does not emanate from those objects. Neither does the soul possess a dim light of its own which brightens upon contact with those shining spheres. Socrates introduces a "third term" to explain the knowing process. Neither "sight by itself" nor what is seen can be considered the source of the "light" which allows seeing and being seen. A "third element" is required, a kind of "connection," for the soul to be able to enter into contemplation and for the ideas to be contemplated. If we compare the process of knowing with the process of seeing, we can affirm that the "colors will remain invisible in the absence of the third thing" and the organ of sight will not be able to utilize its own capabilities.[7]

In order for sight to see effectively and for what is visible actually
to be seen a mediating term is needed which connects and brings
together both "capabilities," binding them together and making
sight—knowing—possible. "You may have the power of vision in
your eyes and try to use it, and color may be there in the objects;
but sight will see nothing and the colors will remain invisible in
the absence of a third thing peculiarly constituted to serve this very
purpose."

This third thing—"light"—does not issue either from sight or
from visible things. Consequently Socrates asks: "And of all the
divinities in the skies is there one whose light, above all the rest,
is responsible for making our eyes see perfectly and making objects
perfectly clear?"[8]

The source and cause of light is the "sun." In the field of genuine
knowledge, it is *agathon*, the solar Goodness which casts its light
on the soul and on intelligible objects, surrounding both and enabling them to see and be seen. The soul's ability to see "is dis-
pensed by the Sun, like a stream flooding the eye."[9]

The Good, then, is the unconditioned condition (anhypotheton)
of knowing.[10] In modern terminology, we would say that the Good
is "transcendental," the unconditioned condition of knowledge. It
is a "transcendent transcendental," however, a "sun" which cannot
be identified either with sight or with visible things. These *receive*
their qualities of seen and seer from the sun. Knowledge is constrained, then, by the condition of that entity which surpasses both
the seer and the seen, constituting the possibility of both. Knowledge in some way is a "gift" received from the solar Goodness, that
"heavenly god" who closes the circle of knowing by the act of
illuminating.

The Good, the soul, and the ideas are the three elements required for knowing: a kind of Goodness able to diffuse its luminous
gift, a kind of soul liberated from material constraints and open to
receive the gift, and an intelligible world free of the shadows that
darken its face, its inner mechanisms, its "articulations."

Without these three elements there can be no knowledge. None
of them can be eliminated without blocking the possibility of

knowledge coming into being. Together, therefore, they make something like a triangle with peculiar characteristics. Each of them is one of the points, and the sides of the triangle are the "ties that bind" these points together. They are made of light.

II

Platonic epistemology thus makes use of three terms to explain the process of knowing. And yet one of the three is out of sync with the others, because it actually makes the relationship and communication between them possible. This one, the Good, opens the circuit of knowing to the extent that it dispenses and originates all "light." The central problem of this epistemology would appear to arise precisely in the passage of the *Republic* which we are now analyzing. The problem is, how can the very source of knowledge, the Good, be known? Can we have any knowledge of the Good?

Knowledge of the "idea of the Good" is Socrates' "most difficult" and dangerous doctrine, and also his "supreme" doctrine.[11] No sooner does an analysis of this idea get underway than Socrates and his friends vacillate and interrupt each other. Because the idea is so difficult to define rationally, they eventually decide to use an "allegory." The problem is that the idea of the Good presupposes every definition and every rational approach. The Good is the ground of the Logos: it is the foundation of the possibility of seeing and being seen. It makes the intelligible world possible and is the condition for conceiving of such a world.[12] In some sense it cannot be an "idea" precisely because it is the condition of all Ideas. All knowledge of the ideas, including knowledge of the Good "as an idea," assumes that the Good is the condition of this very knowledge. As an idea, it is beyond itself. It surpasses the soul, the ideas, and even itself insofar as it is the "idea of the Good."

Plato brilliantly dramatizes the fundamental dilemma of his epistemological inquiry. How can a transcendental be posited which is simultaneously transcendent? What do we know about this thing? And if, when all is said and done, we have a deficient, problematic, "philosophical" knowledge of an "idea" or "essence" that is not commensurate with its enigmatic reality, how can we demand that it be transcendent, that it be the condition of knowledge? What kind of knowledge or preknowledge authorizes us to introduce a third term about which we have merely a confused notion?

To the soul the Good "appears" to be an "idea," indeed, something like the idea of all ideas. But the Good is the condition of this "appearance," and the "condition" itself does not appear, being hidden or absent. What does appear has the status of all "ideas": it is being, *ousia*. But the Good in itself is not *ousia*. Between the Good *par' emon*—the Good which appears to the soul—and the Good *kath' auton*—the Good in itself—a gap opens of which Plato himself had only a vague apprehension. The soul's vision neither takes in nor penetrates the complete density of this difficult object. It does not see into its depths, into its Being. The duality of being and appearance, banished from the world of the ideas, reappears with the Good. There is a gap between its appearance—its "countenance"—and its reality (to the extent that *eidos* and *ousia* are the same in Plato, this reality is not a pure *ousia*). And the soul is ignorant of this reality. It can only "assume" that it exists: it can only postulate it without being totally capable of analyzing it systematically.

This hypothesis nevertheless has a basis which Plato explains in other dialogues, like the *Symposium*. The soul suspects that the Good is an object that exceeds its narrow understanding and vision. It nevertheless pursues it, dogging it within the confines of its intellective activity. The soul is condemned to chase after a "good" which always gets away. It constantly "believes" that it has at last caught it, trapped it with its eyesight or snared it with theory. And yet it escapes from its sight every time it exceeds—and therefore makes possible—any theory. It is condemned to destroy all intellectual apprehension of the good and pursue it beyond all intellection. In this way Plato establishes the limits of his own epistemological configuration: the condition of knowing, to the degree that it transcends or exceeds all actual knowledge, cannot be the object of a "systematic" investigation. Or if it is, it is a defective, incomplete, "philosophical" object. The soul does not fully understand the condition of its knowledge. It only knows it "halfway," the other half—what is "outside" its own boundaries—being something outsized, adequate only to the *sophoi*. But only the gods are wise, not this daimonic creature of the in-between that is the soul. To the soul alone is it given to "covet," to "desire" that object that it knows by suspicion, by conjecture. Eros goes where sight is not able to tread. The impossible knowledge of the Good *kath' auton* is extenuated by a desire which goes beyond the scope of vision, always pushing or leading it beyond itself, shaking it loose from its own theoretical smugness.[13]

The soul is therefore confined to the task of constantly shrinking the "idea" that it has of the "good." It must continually shatter the "outward appearance of the good" which is the only way in which the good presents itself to the soul. It must go beyond this appearance toward a reality it cannot conceive beforehand. This means that sight must be clouded and intelligence obliterated. For this reason mysticism is the only way out of the epistemological dilemma. The good cannot be known or seen in itself, but the infusion of its being, the soul's "wedding" or "copulation" with the Good is possible. In this way the desire to know—Eros—can be satisfied.[14] But it is a precarious satisfaction: this blind, Dionysian copulation with the Good does not sustain theoretical insight. Knowledge and mystical union are irreconcilable. The soul's "movement" derives from this fact. It no longer loiters in physical bodies: it anxiously runs after a Good that totally exceeds it. Possession and understanding are no longer bound up with each other as they are in the knowledge of objects. Knowledge of the appearance of the Good, of what it lets show (the idea of the Good) does not lead to knowledge of its inner reality: it does not see into that reality. This is why the soul is "philosophical" but not knowledgeable. The epistemological problems raised by Platonism demand this precarious kind of knowledge called philosophy.

III

These, then, are the epistemological problems raised by Platonism. The knowledge we now call "philosophy," that is, knowledge which studies the conditions of the possibility of knowing, turns out to be philosophical in the etymological sense (which is its meaning in Plato). It is a deficient kind of science which supports and brings together two activities which in the general scheme of things shine on their own: a kind of knowledge requiring both a dialectical approach that leads to genuine, rational knowledge, and the mystical way—the way of union—leading to the "abandonment" of sight and blind infusion of solar Goodness. A kind of knowledge which upholds theoria and eros simultaneously. A kind of knowledge imbued with a "philosophical eros" that extenuates its blindness with a science it knows to be deficient. In the *Symposium* the philosophy of Eros is explained; in the *Phaedrus*, the eroticism of philosophy.

These problems continue in Neoplatonism, in the Middle Ages and today, making it possible for "scholastic rationalism" and "mysticism" to enrich each other. Both tendencies can exist within the same thinker without contradiction. It is only in retrospect that we notice a difference or separation, a possible "contradiction" in this sense. Because it is usually impossible for us to travel this broad road of Platonism we project our difficulty on a past which lived comfortably with problems requiring both approaches. As soon as we enter the "modern" period the echoes of these problems begin to be muffled, because the structure of epistomology, its configuration, is gradually reorganized. The epistemological triangle starts breaking apart, and an unsuspected configuration appears which defines knowledge by different principles. The requirements for possessing knowledge have profoundly altered.

2. The Light of Reason

Now the soul, in order to obtain genuine knowledge, must also free itself of the evidence of the senses and the "deceiving judgment of the imagination." It is nevertheless enough for the soul to free itself of the prejudices or "idols" which disturb its unique activity: thinking. The soul is a substance whose nature is thinking. And in order to think, a structured process must be followed. This process goes calmly and gradually, with control and taking the obstacles into account, from simplicity to complexity. The starting point is those *semences de verité* which are the natural truths, truths which present themselves spontaneously whenever the soul extricates itself from the "madness" and sleepwalking induced by the imagination. All true sciences feed off these "seeds": they make up a single science, *la Sagesse humaine* (human discernment). At bottom they shelter certain representations or discernible "ideas" about which Reason can no longer harbor any doubt whatsoever.[15]

> No one of the sciences is ever other than (the outcome of) human discernment, which remains always one and the same, however different be the things to which it is directed, being no more altered by them than is the light of the sun by the variety of things it illuminates.[16]

This human Knowing, the knowledge possessed by an enlightened Reason, no longer requires the "third term" in order to "know." The fire that illuminates it is internal to it and to the very act of knowing. The epistemological triangle is shattered. This kind of Reason no longer needs a solar Goodness to awaken it to knowledge by infusing it with "light." Nor does the "self-evident idea" require the intervention of solar light in order to "be visible," that is, to activate the faculty of being seen. The solar vertex is now split into two sustaining points: seer and seen take control of light, are light. Reason is "luminous," images are "evident" and "clear" in their own right. Reason and representation are the only terms of Descartes' epistemological configuration. The "unconditioned condition" of knowledge, however, the "source of light" is not taken over by either if they are considered separate from each other. Light will belong to the sight or "intuition" that takes notice of an evident representation or idea. It will be the possession of Reason—it will be a kind of Reason which intuits the truth by simple inspection, a kind of reason possessing the seeds of truth, that is, the self-evident ideas that constitute the foundation and substance of knowledge.

On the one hand, the ideas that the mind forms when it actually thinks are clear, simple, distinct, and self-evident in their own right. They hold in themselves the criteria of their own truth and certainty. Their own self-evidence is the condition of possibility and guarantee that their knowledge is authentic. They are thus unquestionable: within them is the fire and light that illuminate them and make them visible. They are visible and transparent in their own right, but only to the kind of sight that discovers its own ability to see and inspect within itself, once it is free of confusion and error. Visible only to a rational kind of sight which finds proof of its existence in what it actually sees, asking no help from outside. On the contrary, it has by its very nature met the requirements and conditions for knowledge.

In fact complete transparency reigns between intuiting sight and intuited idea. Both are luminous, and their light does not stem from a third element. *The internal fire that closes the circuit of knowledge without the intervention of third parties is lighted in the very act of seeing and being seen.*

The act of thinking itself might likewise seem to resemble a "self-evident" idea like that primordial, unquestionable idea that puts an end at last to the assault of doubt. The mind will be, in its own perception, a self-evident idea and a transparent representation. Reason will see itself. The unconditioned condition will easily rise to the level of a "representation" without requiring the pursuit of any "supreme object" whose nature it is to flee from its reach. The mystical way is thus blocked: reason will be sufficient unto itself for the purposes of knowing. As Locke confesses from the heart of the Cartesian epistemological configuration:

> It will be no excuse to an idle and untoward servant who would not attend his business by candle light, to plead that he had not broad sunshine. The Candle that is set up in us shines bright enough for all our purposes.[17]

Knowledge must satisfy itself and not "despair," as skepticism does, within its own boundaries. It must not refer to any greater object, beyond the reach of reason, even if this object has the prestige conferred by theology. Mystical union becomes separated from the epistemological configuration. God becomes an object of knowledge to the extent that he is a "self-evident idea" possessed by reason. And even though the notion of the Deity's function is still ambiguous in Descartes (God is both a "self-evident idea" of Reason and the guarantee of this self-evidence) and although a strict Cartesian would point out on the basis of Arnault's criteria that Descartes' reasoning is circular, he would not try to find proof of the self-evidence of ideas outside the ideas themselves and their own self-evident nature. Ideas are guaranteed by their self-evidence. Reason is guaranteed by its own introspection and intuition.[18] Seer and seen are transparent. The tie that binds them together is definitely some kind of light, but not the *epyrriton* of the solar Goodness, the third term of the Platonic triangle. This light is immanent to both seer and seen. It lodges within Reason, within its internal seeds of truth, and its ability to watch intently. The epistemological configuration only breaks down at that moment when a criterion more reliant than "evidence" is found, at the moment in which this approach is suspected of "dogmatism," when we awake from our dogmatic slumber. . . . At that moment we will seek an "unconditioned condition" for these same "representations" of reason which carry within themselves the anhypothetical guarantee and condition of the "rationalist" configuration. The linear equilibrium between the two terms will be disrupted when one or the other of these elements plunges to the "depths" or "foundation" which make knowledge possible.

3. Obscurities of Reason

The epistemological configuration we have described enables us to understand the full impact of Descartes' doctrine. Knowledge will be built on a solid foundation, on the "seeds of truth." Reason will always start out with simples, with clear and self-evident ideas. By comparing their various representations, it will gradually form

complex ideas or deduce others which are less than self-evident.
It will always proceed methodically, working from simplicity to
complexity, from what is self-evident to what is less evident. Avoiding haste and procrastination, it will never take shortcuts or look
for quick solutions. It will be careful to ignore the advice of that
untrustworthy advisor, the imagination—a constant source of error
and judgments which, far from being correct, are merely probable.
In this way reason will make all possible representations crystal
clear: it will make them its private realm of knowledge. It will
clarify the representations we have of celestial and earthly bodies.
It will clear up every field of knowledge from geometry to theology.
It is the job of the post-Cartesian philosophies, all of them based
on the same epistemological configuration, to bring this about. The
convergence of "rationalism" and "empiricism" in the philosophy
of the Enlightenment bears fruit in the "general science of ideas"
of the late eighteenth and earlier nineteenth centuries. This science
is "ideology," the attempt to bring the science of a century and a
half together in encyclopedic fashion after first clarifying all of the
ideas that human reason has represented to itself.

This mammoth edifice can stand in place only if the rules of the
game are observed. If the boundaries imposed by the method are
crossed or any of the cornerstones of the epistemological configuration shift position, the entire structure of knowledge comes
tumbling down. At what price, then, does it achieve its stability
and permanence, its rationality? In virtue of what "excess"?

Pascal provides an answer. This kind of knowledge subsists on
an excess which is diametrically opposed to skepticism. "Deux
excès: exclure la raison, n'admettre que la raison."[19]

The counterpart of this excess is the penury of Cartesian method,
champion of a methodology which models its procedures on geometry and is not suited for sounding the depths of the "human
heart." In vain will the empiricists describe the genesis of ideas in
human understanding, and the rationalists will attempt in vain to
separate immanent ideas from the faculty of reason. Neither group
finds "man" but rather a shred of him in the form of human un-

derstanding or reason. What about feelings, what about the human heart? They, too, are analyzed, of course. Both Locke and Descartes, for instance, consider "dreams" to be senseless, aleatory clusters of representations and ideas arbitrarily linked together. The same holds true, they find, for the faculty of imagination, the movements of the heart and the emotions. They analyze and pass judgment on these as if they were the residue of thought and reason, as if they were odd mixtures and backslidings. Pascal, however, tries to bring this confusion of heart and mind, of imagination and reason, together into a whole. Where Cartesianism specifies, divides, and splits apart, Pascal finds a unified whole. This whole is called "man."

But how can we know man? How study him? The "geometrical" approach is no longer sufficient: at bottom, it is useless. Will we, then, follow the Cartesian precept of "order"? "Nulle science humaine ne le peut garder." How can we use a geometrical method or procedure to know something that has its "own order" which by comparison with geometry is truly "chaotic"? How arrive at a clear, self-evident notion of the human heart in all its versatility and messiness, the ultimate enigma for human reason?[20]

The "science of man" must accommodate itself to its subject. It cannot proceed methodically in the manner of the *esprit géométrique* and pure reason. On the contrary, it must find recruits among those values that Cartesianism represses: *esprit de finesse*, imagination, fantasy, the turmoil of the heart, emotional distress.[21]

Man can only be the object of science to the extent that science is "surpassed" and done away with. Man is the object of science only if we step outside the realm of science. Man marks the very boundary of Cartesianism: the more the latter moves toward the former, the faultier it becomes. Its trajectory begins to resemble that of the Platonic soul, in search of its own overflowing ground. In Pascal's interpretation, man is the cornerstone that shatters Cartesianism. Pascal has not entirely broken with Cartesianism, however: it remains in place in his epistemological configuration. This is why he restricts himself to proposing the "anti-method" as

a means of access to "man"—that is, the exact opposite of the path
of reason, the descent into those areas that reason had repressed:
the emotions and the heart.[22]

Pascal's "human science" does not yet represent the breakdown
or disintegration of the Cartesian epistemological configuration.[23]
It simply implies an "anti-science" which is the inverse of the common knowledge. It is scientific in the sense that it is anti-scientific.
It is a science which marks the boundary of the science by pointing,
geometrically, toward a distant land that is the realm of "non-science."[24] "Man" is definitely starting to take shape on the epistemological horizon. But he does not take up residence there or
occupy any space in the epistemological configuration. He is rather
a reference point—he stakes out the borderline of epistemology.
He is the "invisible," inner transcendence: he is precisely what the
acknowledged "problems" repress in order to bring out the fron-
tiers that de-limit it. Later, beginning with Kant, this "invisible"
quantity will become visible. Man suddenly appears in a new configuration, and contemporary philosophy is born.

4. The Copernican Revolution

Critical philosophy appears to take up the issues of Cartesianism,
enacting the "synthesis" between "rationalism" and "empiricism"
which is implicit in the Enlightenment. The "critique of pure
reason" thus becomes an attempt to consolidate the Cartesian and
post-Cartesian epistemological configurations. To the analysis of
the "physiognomy" of human understanding begun by empiricism,
to the rationalist dream of a *mathesis universalis* that includes
both the general science of signs and the general science of ideas
(ideology), critical philosophy adds the study of the "conditions of
possibility" of those representations. It ascertains those "a priori
forms" of emotions and understanding which set the boundaries
of these same representations. Critical philosophy apparently puts
the finishing touches on the palace of Reason by investigating its
boundaries. It thus fulfills Locke's intention of studying the scope

and range of human understanding, a project which had already
been outlined by Descartes.

In reality, this investigation follows a peculiar route: these "conditions" of knowledge, these "forms" are not yet the ultimate goal
of the inquiry. The "critique of pure reason" turns entirely on
"transcendental Deduction." In this trajectory it becomes quite
clear that the inquiry will not be completed by an inventory of the
"forms": these, for their part, must be "deduced" from the basis
or "ground" which constitutes their "condition of possibility."

Now, this ground does not issue from any of the structural elements of the Cartesian configuration. Descartes' "je pense" is not
after all a representation or "self-evident" idea or the clearest and
most obvious paradigm demonstrating the remaining representations. The ground is the "transcendental subject" which synthesizes
all the representations, seeing itself as a representation or "object"
while at the same time knowing—if only on an intuitive level—
that it is a "subject," something different from all those things
which are represented, something different from itself to the extent
that it is a representation.

The epistemological configuration that thus takes shape has two
faces. On the one hand there is the "transcendental subject," the
unconditioned condition of all knowledge, the foundation or *Grund*
from which arise all of the "forms" that make the representations
possible. On the other hand there are the "forms" of feeling and
understanding which make up the classifying equipment by which
representations are ranked and organized and become the condition
of possibility of "objects." "Subject" and "object" are the only
terms of this configuration.

Now, the thinking "subject" itself becomes an "object" of the
transcendental consciousness. The subject *knows* that it thinks and
understands: it recognizes *itself* to be the condition of knowledge.
The subject stands before itself as "object." It is an object in its
own eyes, a more radical and primordial Self which is always in the
background, never showing itself as a "representation" because it
is the basis of representation, what makes all knowledge. This
primordial subject does not "make itself known" in the Kantian

beginnings of critical philosophy. It is postulated or assumed but not openly recognized. Fichte challenged Kant's timidity by affirming the intuitive, primordial kind of knowledge that was more radical than knowledge obtained from "representations," that is, the Self's knowledge of itself, the Self's primordial reflection on itself which precedes the knowledge or reflection of itself as "object." It is a knowledge that is also "possession."

On the basis of these two elements, the subject and the object, the set of problems expands into the following issues: a primordial subject which has an immediate knowledge of itself; a subject which takes the form of an "object" of representation; a world of "objects" which is known by the transcendental subject's special ways of knowing.

The subject is consequently an object and is not an object. To the extent that it is the condition of possibility or the anhypothetical basis of objectivity, it is not an object. It becomes an object as soon as it shows itself "systematically" to its own perceiving consciousness. True objects, on the other hand, are trapped in the circuit of subjectivity, without which they are not knowable and cannot even be objects. They are different from that original, primordial subjectivity which is always "beyond" objectivity.

This "primordial subject" evidently becomes a fleeting thing. It almost seems to run away from the possibility of being understood, following a trajectory like the Platonic Good. But in fact this primordial subject is known, only in an immediate, original way. Plato said that light could not shine out from the human eye. For Fichte the brilliant fire, the source of light and the condition of understanding, is part of the human Self, and the Self has immediate knowledge of itself.

The problem that later philosophy was to pose for itself is here in embryonic form: What kind of knowledge is this? What kind of knowledge does the self have of itself if it is not "objective"? These are the issues of contemporary philosophy.

The Cartesian epistemological configuration, however, has been shattered in the process. The anhypothetical condition or prerequisite of knowledge is no longer the self-evidence of Ideas. The solar blaze no longer fuels the apprehension of the unambiguous idea. This is not the act by which reason testifies to its diaphanous nature or thought intuits the self-evident idea. This configuration is now challenged on the grounds that it is "dogmatic" and "formalist." The unconditioned condition is "beyond" all representation. The unconditioned condition of all objective knowledge is the transcendental self-conscious subject.

With this, the so-called "Copernican revolution" of philosophy takes place. All science, all knowledge has its source not in a transcendent Good or the immanent evidence of intuition but in a "transcendental consciousness" which recognizes and knows and grounds itself in its own reflection on itself and in its own forms and configurations, which are the possibility of objective knowledge. From this moment on philosophy is "subjectivist" or it is not at all. Fichte pointed out the dilemma: either one holds that the ground of the system of science is the Self (subjective idealism) or one falls victim to dogmatism, in which, as Hegel says, self-consciousness disappears instead of asserting itself.[25] The Hegelian synthesis of "substance and subject" is a refinement of this notion. The "transcendental" problems, the raising of "self-consciousness" to the level of importance of a foundation (in Hegel, the mind's self-consciousness in and for itself), are nevertheless a topic and *point d'appui* of all philosophical inquiry.

5. Man Appears on the Scene

These, in general terms, are the three epistemological configurations underlying the three types of philosophical inquiry (Platonism, Cartesianism, Kantianism). We notice the same unchanging elements in all three—the knower and the known—but these alter their *value* as a function of a third element, the unconditioned condition that enables the knower to know and the known to be known. This unconditioned condition shifts position in each of the three constellations, thereby changing the relationships between the remaining elements. Each of these shifts implies an alteration in the structure of the configuration—implies, in fact, the passage from one configuration to the next.

In Platonism the "third"—unconditioned—"term" was *outside* the knower and the known, while in Cartesianism it was placed on the same level of these two. It was built into the relationship between knower and known. In Kantianism, by contrast, the relationship is weighted in favor of the knower, who is elevated to the status of an unconditioned. Where in Platonism the unconditioned was external and *transcendent*, in Cartesianism and Kantianism it is *immanent* to both the knower and the known.

Given this, is it possible ultimately to pose the basic question of this essay: in which of these configurations does "man" finally appear as a relevant aspect of the whole? Can we discover a configuration in which man is welcome as an unconditioned condition of knowledge? In which of these configurations will philosophy be or tend to be a "philosophy of man"?

"Man" does not appear in the Platonic configuration at all. In neither the *Phaedo*, the *Phaedrus*, nor the *Laws* does "soul" have any anthropological connotation whatsoever. "Man" is a *meikton* which can be known only when the harsh prison of the body is left behind. The soul, guided by *Nous*—the principle of intellection and the source of life—is what can have knowledge. Nor does man appear in Cartesianism. We have already seen how resistant the Cartesian approach is to a deep analysis of human dimensions like feeling, emotions, and the imagination. Man took the form of an "invisible presence" in that configuration, something repressed so that it can give testimony to its own shape, its own boundaries. Understood in his entirety, man could be neither subject nor object of knowledge. This is why the only thinker in the Cartesian tradition to take man into account—Pascal— succeeded merely in drawing attention to the limitations and instability of the problems themselves.

With Kantianism, however, something else happens. The Copernican Revolution indicates that the only relevant way to pose the problem of knowledge is to search for the conditions of possibility of that knowledge. And this search culminates in the discovery of

an anhypotheton, that is, "transcendental subjectivity." Now this
subject, which at the beginning of Kantianism could attain no other
knowledge of itself than that of a "representation" whose theoretical life was cut off from "practical life," is finally endowed with
a structure by Fichte. The duality of a subject verging on knowledge
but cut off from a subject bordering on action is destroyed by a
higher synthesis. The subject needs some form of "action" or "primordial praxis" in order to understand and know. This action is
already a primary means of knowing: a primordial means which
lays the basis for the possibility of knowing. The subject knows
himself, intuits and "affirms" himself in this primordial action by
virtue of which he "establishes" himself as an object of "systematic"
knowledge. The subject knows something about himself which is
more basic than his own representation, his own "system," his own
"objectivity." He knows himself in acting, in praxis, in doing (*Tun*).

Beginning with Fichte, all of man's dimensions begin to congeal
around a common origin and point of dispersal which is the subject's
primordial (cognitive-practical) praxis. Theory and praxis both get
their start in this unified space. And soon after these problems are
fully mature, with Feuerbach, the center of dispersal at last shines
its light into all the nooks and crannies of the human condition,
even those most inaccessible, resistant to reason and ignominious.
Man will not merely be a being who thinks and acts but a being
who meets his own basic needs, who works and reproduces. He
will be that creature which (pardoning the redundancy) "human-
izes" all of his actions, even the most commonplace, like eating,
drinking, and procreating. Man is at last complete, but his completeness radiates from a central point which is always his self-
consciousness, his own primordial knowledge of himself. This center is the "transcendental subject." Transcendental philosophy
therefore necessarily implies an anthropology. Man must hold the
rank of transcendental subject.

Moreover, this human completeness will be "thinkable" in its
entirety. All of man's dimensions become the substance of knowledge without there being any danger of paradox, as in Pascal. Man
likewise draws on all of his powers, on all of the dimensions of his

being, in the act of knowing. He follows the inverse path of Platonism and Cartesianism: instead of freeing himself from his body, instead of repressing his imagination and his emotions, he glows with the light stamped on his (subjective) core, the light of the outflowing of the completeness of his being.

Because the "sun," Plato's unconditioned, now appears in the very interior of man, in that area of retreat where man reflects on himself and arrives at primordial knowledge of himself. The sun is "thinkable," and the peril of infinite regress, always present in Plato, is eliminated.

What Pascal set forth to accomplish without being able to carry through would now seem to be feasible: a science of man, a knowledge of man's every dimension. The "man" who was the cornerstone upon which Cartesian science shattered will now be the cornerstone that guarantees the triumph of post-Kantian philosophy. Man is completely enveloped by critical inquiry: he shows himself to be the authentic "transcendental subject." The question "Who is it who knows?" now becomes entwined with the question "What is man?" The answer is "Only man really knows, because man alone possesses self-consciousness." Before man alone does the world of objects acquire a profile. Man holds the secret to all power, which always flows out from him, from his unique way of thinking and of knowing. Kant says over and over again that the limits placed on knowledge are valid "only for us, for men." The same is true of the conditions of knowing—that is, those conditions of knowledge discovered by criticism to be "human" conditions. Criticism demands an "anthropology."

In this configuration, then, man becomes the transcendental anhypothetical subject of knowledge. He is an unregulated subject who undertakes the primordial action that grounds all "objects." He is in all events the unconditioned condition of knowledge. The moment is drawing near when the young Marx will summarize this configuration in the saying: "man is the root."

The primordial task of this set of problems is thus specified: to know man. Of necessity the task develops in a number of directions.

To the extent that man is a self-conscious subject containing within himself a primordial but not strictly "objective" knowledge, the ways and means of studying this elemental human dimension must be investigated. To the extent that man becomes an "object" of his own reflection he must be studied with the means and methods customarily used in the study of "objects." First and foremost, man develops two lines of investigation, two methods which, although they seem contradictory, in reality complement each other. Man must be known "in depth," in the dimension of his liberty, his original praxis, his self-consciousness—that is, in his subjective dimension. On the other hand, he must be known in his "positive" dimension as something "placed," as a "positum" or "phenomenon" which appears before the conscious mind. He must be studied as other phenomena are studied and with the same methods. He must be known in his "objective" dimension. Man is simultaneously subject and object, thus requiring a method of study which gets to the bottom of two dimensions. And these two directions or methods make constant demands on him: thus it is possible for a "philosophy of man" or "philosophical anthropology" to come into being which inquires into the "internal" dimension of man while at the same time making use—and demanding the use—of "positivist" techniques. With them come into being a variety of "human sciences" which study the "exterior" of man, the form he takes in the eyes of (human!) consciousness as if he were an empirical object, while at the same time requiring a philosophical "grounding." The complicity of epistemology and anthropology implies the complicity of the philosophy of man and the "human sciences." Every discourse which refuses to value this complicity will be condemned: every science, like every morality, represents a danger of "dehumanizing" man, converting him into a mere object or "thing." From Fichte to Sartre, this danger hounds the problems that philosophy poses for itself.

The third and final direction: along with this kind of anthropology and the human sciences, there should be a discipline which studies both the subjective and the objective dimensions in all of their

mutual interplay and implications. This discipline—*dialectics*—
studies precisely the movement or process created by the subjective
and objective elements in the heart of human completeness. This
movement or process will be understood to be human *history*, man's
ongoing creation of himself, his continuous objectification of himself on the basis of the primordial praxis and the subject's continuous reappropriation of the objectified self.

If Fichte attempted to systematize the elemental dimension of
the human Self and the primordial knowledge which is manifested
in this dimension, in his phenomenology Hegel studied the dialectical process that constitutes the historical plot of man's spiritual
completeness in its subjective and objective aspects.

Anthropology, dialectics, and the human sciences are thus the
three relevant directions of study within the configurations opened
up by Kant. Anthropology studies man as the constituent subject
of knowledge as well as of all kinds of "creation": man as maker
of signs, values, means of production, customs, laws. The human
sciences on the other hand study the results of man's primordial
activity: languages, social and cultural systems, etc. Finally, dialectics studies the relationship between "subject" and "object," serving
as a bridge between anthropology and the human sciences and
studying the mutual relationships between the objects studied by
these sciences. Dialectics enables us to discover and describe the
"humanist" program in the epistemological configuration, whose
object is to study man in his completeness. In practice, dialectics
does not limit itself to man's dimensions as constituent subject or
constituted object. Rather it investigates the "concrete reality" constituted by subject and object.

PART II: HEGEMONY

1. Consummation of the Copernican Revolution

"But what is the essential difference between man and the brute?" The answer to this question, which begins *The Essence of Christianity*, points to a commonplace inherent in the problems posed by the post-Kantian philosophy to which Feuerbach subscribed. "The most simple, general, and also the most popular answer to this question is—consciousness; but consciousness in the strict sense. . . . present only in a being to whom his species, his essential nature, is an object of thought." This difference does not stem simply from the fact of man's scientific aptitude, science being "the cognizance of species," in the Aristotelian sense, but rather from the fact that man applies this aptitude first and foremost to a specific species, *his own*. Man alone has the capacity to be conscious of himself as species or essence. This capacity is the guarantee of all his reflective and scientific activity, in addition to what sets him basically apart from the animals. "Only a being to whom his own species, his own nature, is an object of thought, can make the essential nature of other things an object of thought."[26] This basic, primordial consciousness that man has of himself is the starting point of his conscious awareness of other objects. Science being the cognizance of species, this "preconsciousness" allows and makes possible all science.

Feuerbach's answer thus relates fully to the problems identified by critical philosophy. We shall soon see to what extent it highlights these problems and rids them of ambiguity. Regarding this question, however, Feuerbach has indicated a radical discontinuity with precritical answers. For Descartes and the "Port-Royalists" the essential difference between man and animal was man's undeniable possession of language. The existence of rational language and the ability to express thought with a limited number of sounds, to create an endless discourse into which ideas are woven in a meaningful order, possibly to communicate these ideas to other men—this is the difference between man and beast. The ability to think in a way that can be communicated by language could not be found in animals, which are ruled by their instincts and shaped by their environments. Man, on the contrary, was able continually to create new discourses, submitting only to the rules that governed their creation.[27]

Feuerbach understands this difference between man and beast in quite a different way. It is not "thought" or the ability to give verbal expression to ideas or the possibility of bringing representations together in the composition of ordered, rational discourse that distinguishes man from the animals. It is neither thought nor the fundamental attitude of rising from contemplation of the specific, individual objects of sense perception to general concepts. The difference is more radical, if you will: it is rooted in the undeniable fact, in Feuerbach's view, that man is *conscious of himself as a species*. Man possesses foreknowledge, basic and original awareness, and this is the condition of knowledge and of all the sciences. It is knowing himself as essence and species. Man possesses his own essence as first object and initial endowment. This marks his difference from other beings: it is the condition of the possibility of knowing, of knowledge and of science.

The second point is important: in this way the post-Kantian revolution comes together and acquires a definite form. The Copernican Revolution comes full circle. The search for "conditions of possibility," for a priori knowledge, points in the end to that being in whom it is grounded and from whom the ability to know is developed. In the end man is clearly seen to be the authentic transcendental subject. It is also established that this being possesses an intimate knowledge of his very essence. Man knows himself: this original reflection is at the root of all subsequent knowledge. Science, that "system of knowledge" which idealism tried to "ground," in the end discovers its elemental a priori, its ultimate point of departure, its "presupposition"—man. And man has this prerogative for a very clear reason: he has primordial foreknowledge of his own essence.

This means that man knows himself completely. He knows his entire complex, generic being and not merely a single aspect of his being, like reason at the expense of emotion, or theory at the expense of action. The Kantian waverings have been quieted. The paradoxical nature of human science as proposed by Pascal has been avoided. Man is no longer a transitory phenomenon, as in Pascal, that cannot be studied "geometrically," and that can only be known as a form of non-science, by the applications of methods which Cartesianism suppresses. Man now stands forth in his completeness with the status of an object of knowledge. Not an isolated part of him but his very essence: "to a complete man belong the power of thought, the power of will, the power of affection." This is the divine Trinity of "reason, love, force of will," which are "perfections—the perfections of the human being—nay, more, they are absolute perfections of being."[28] This trinity now calmly assumes the status of an object of knowledge, without creating any Pascalian paradox and without the shakiness inherited from the ponderous tradition of Cartesianism that is found in Kant.

This is why Feuerbach can flatly state: "I have regarded *man* as the criterion of truth, and not this or that founder of a system."[29] The problems first posed by Kant are thus clarified and rid of tacit complicity with Cartesianism. Man is the privileged object of knowledge. He is also the condition of possibility or *Grund* of knowledge to the extent that he is known in his "entirety," as a "complete man" and not a slice or extract of man. And this complete man is a man who thinks, of course, but who also acts, unifying the life of theory and everyday activities, manifesting his essence in the entire range of his pursuits—a being who eats, drinks, creates, and procreates as well. The complete man is an empirical datum, a fact plainly visible to eyes that know how to see, legible to those who know how to read. He is neither an abstraction nor a caricature of himself. Feuerbach counters Hegelian thought with a ground of knowing that is also the fundamental datum of science: man as he actually is, a creature of skin and bones—not a fiction of his own imagination. For Feuerbach man is not dreamt up in the *internal* ravings of mental speculation: rather, he is understood once knowledge, purified by the *hydrotherapy* of cold reason, turns to "things in themselves" and pays strict attention to them. Knowledge should turn to the *outside*, it should leave its mystical-speculative ravings behind and know things that can be seen. Among the latter, perhaps the most visible of all—also the most prone to being hidden away— is man.[30]

The methodological consequence of this argument is as follows: on the one hand, man is a *datum*, a fact, a concrete object. He is therefore a scientific object, to the extent that science spurns the imaginary creations of speculation and reason rejects the speculative mirage which considers what is "ideal" to be "real." On the other hand, this datum has a unique status. It is the initial, elemental datum: it appears in consciousness before all other data. Man is himself the first object of human knowledge. This datum functions as the starting point for all knowledge. Therefore, there is no science without knowledge of man, without "anthropology." Anthropology is the science par excellence.[31] Its object is the condition of possibility and the a priori of all other objects. Through it we can have knowledge which is both previous and "internal." Man is an "external datum," but only to the extent that he takes shape within himself. He is an "object among objects," a thing among things, to the extent that he has already assumed the form of an object in his own subjectivity, that is, to the extent that he *is* this very Subject and knows that he is.

The man who knows is the man who knows himself, whence his privileged position in the universe of science. Scientific study and reasoning always presuppose a thinking and suffering being who carries through with his studying and his suffering. All knowledge therefore bears man's signature. Science always demands anthropology.

In this way Feuerbach traces the two methods within a kind of science which requires "grounding" in anthropology. Any analysis of Feuerbach is therefore simultaneously "empirical" and "historico-philosophical."[32] Anthropology, the primordial science, thus acquires the status of a "primordial philosophy" (a first philosophy, metaphysics). *The ancient prestige of the "science in search of itself," concerned with first principles and ultimate questions, is now taken over by anthropology.* But this science must simultaneously investigate its object—man—as both "object" and "condition" of objectivity," as "external thing," "datum," "empirical fact," and as the transcendental subject that makes possible the opening toward objectivity, toward the constitution of all objects.[33] Anthropology must therefore combine a rigorous analysis of "facts" with the in-depth study of that particular "fact" which constitutes the first *datum* and the condition of appearance of other "data." Man must be studied by empirical methods. But to the extent that he is the condition of all experience, man must be studied by a science of fundamentals, a first philosophy that uncovers the essence and meaning of man. This science, anthropology, cannot as yet have the same epistemological status as the hard sciences. It is the science at the base of all others, the science that guarantees and makes possible the evolution of all science.

Feuerbach thus consummates the "Copernican Revolution" by establishing man as the transcendental subject and the privileged, primordial object of knowledge, the condition of objectivity. He puts anthropology on the footing of a first science and a first philosophy by directing the search for a *Grund* toward the essence of man. Fichte's "introduction to the system of science" begins with the Socratic exhortation to know oneself.[34] Feuerbach heeds this call and gives it expression, claiming that it is the true theme of his book.[35] Unlike Socrates' exhortation, however, this knowledge should not lead to the conclusion that "I only know that I know nothing," the statement that inaugurated "philosophy" in the Platonic sense of a science that can desire but never really know its own "anhypothetical Ground." The exhortation "know thyself" in Feuerbach leads to knowledge in all of its fullness. The philosopher—the anthropologist—is at last a "wise man." Hegel's goal of converting the "love of knowledge" into "knowing itself" is reached. The "anhypothetical ground" of all knowledge is now seen to be a knowable object. The gods are no longer the only wise men, as Socrates held, to the exclusion of man. Man may now be wise, but only because he has been elevated to the category of God, the one and only God. The "gods of religion" are projections of the deity man. Man is now the ground of his knowledge, but the ground is susceptible to being known. We have come an immense distance since Socrates and Platonism: philosophy is now a "science," and the "know thyself" no longer leads to a kind of ignorance but to the all-embracing knowledge of man as a complete being. For Feuerbach, nevertheless, man was the only God.[36]

2. Philosophical Anthropology

Since Feuerbach, then, anthropology has aimed to bring to light the *essence* of man which lies buried beneath a mountain of deceiving representations generated as much by philosophy as by religion. The line of inquiry indicated by *The Essence of Christianity* was to be fully realized in *philosophical anthropology*. This discipline has a twofold task: in the first place, as in Feuerbach's work, it must carry out the hydrotherapeutic task, in the Baconian sense, of "purging" the deceiving representations and graven images that men make of their own essence. Secondly, it must provide a rigorous definition of this essence.

This is why philosophical anthropology should begin by taking inventory of the notions that man has developed about himself in the course of time. The variety and independence of these notions is clear evidence that our consciousness and knowledge of who we *are* is insecure, be it the notion of man forged by Judaeo-Christianity, the idea put forth by Greek philosophy, or the view implicit to the latest stages of logical positivism in Darwin and Freud. Max Scheler expands this list to include five representations.[37] Their discrepancies and unilateral nature lead him to conclude: "Thus we have a scientific, a philosophical and a theological anthropology in complete separation from each other. We do not have a unified idea of man."[38] Cassirer arrives at the same conclusion, that despite the positive contributions to the *autognosis* of our condition made by Socrates, Saint Augustine, and Pascal, the end result is the same.[39] There is a positive outcome to this process, however:

as Max Scheler points out, after ten thousand years of "history" our age is the *first* in which man is wholly and completely "problematic." We do not know what man is, but we acknowledge our ignorance.[40] In other words: only in the present is there a genuine set of *problems* revolving around man.

Through all of the notions which man has historically created about himself it is clear that we have a fragmented representation of ourselves. Each notion systematically approaches a single aspect of man's being, whether the "logos" of the Greeks or the "vital," psychophysical component of modern science. An overall idea of man's many dimensions is nevertheless lacking. All of the representations we have typify one dimension alone. Philosophical anthropology, on the other hand, should present all of these dimensions as a synthesis, offering a unified vision of man, thus abolishing once and for all the outmoded dualisms, affirming the identity of body and soul.[41] This means challenging the Cartesian notion of man as a precarious unity of two substances and criticizing the naturalistic conceptions that *reduce* man to his vital condition. It means affirming the integral unity of life and spirit and the way in which these two components of human nature mutually fertilize each other. The problem of man's essence is thus seen to be the problem of human *completeness*. Pascal's aspiration can now be fulfilled: the transcendental revolution led to an inquiry into human nature to the extent that it entailed clarifying the very problem of knowledge. Beginning with Fichte the unstable synthesis of theoretical and practical reason hinted at by Kant in his *Critique of Judgment* comes into being. The free human Self is simultaneously the center of energy and the unfolding of the practical cognitive faculty. Feuerbach at last undertakes a systematic investigation of "man" as center of this energy; his trinity is finally "thinkable." Philosophical anthropology limits itself to expanding horizons of what is "thinkable," offering an even more complete image of "the complete man," challenging the reductionist views of science, speculative philosophy, and religion, and incorporating their achievements into a unitary concept.

The problem of man's essence again raises the question of how man specifically differs from all other beings in the universe. This entails "[suggesting] a few conclusions that deal with the nature of man in relation to animal and plant and with man's unique metaphysical place in the universe." The word "man," however, as well as the concept, presents "a deceptive ambiguity": "it signifies the particular morphological characteristics of man as a subclass of the vertebrates and mammals" (this is the *systematic, scientific* notion of man). But the word also signifies "the essential nature of man in contrast to the first concept defined within the context of natural science."[42] The specific difference of man, his essence, should be looked for in a way that corresponds to the second meaning because, regarding the first meaning, man does not oppose but rather gathers together and synthesizes the psychophysical grades of being: the affective (plant) impulse which is the lowest spiritual grade, followed by instinct, associative memory, and even the practical intelligence of the higher animals. On the scale of living things man does not differ qualitatively from other beings. The difference is one of grade, of the greater complexity and perfection of all of the traits mentioned above.[43] In this sense not even intelligence is a valid standard for telling man apart from the animals; consequently, it is of no use in identifying man's essence. At this point we "come to the problem that is crucial for our inquiry. . . . One side would reserve intelligence and choice for man and deny them to the animal. This view, in fact, affirms that there is an essential, qualitative difference." Others deny that such a difference exists. Max Scheler himself holds with the second view, but he specifies that man's uniqueness is not a function of intelligence or activity, since his essence "transcends what we call 'life' in the most general sense . . . (including) the particular mode of life called psyche." His difference is that he has a spirit, "whose center of action . . . appears within a finite mode of being we call 'person.'"[44]

Man is different from the animals and all the other residents of the universe because he possesses "a special function of knowledge which [spirit] alone can provide." Because he is a spiritual being, man in effect experiences "existential liberation from the organic world." He is "'free from the environment' or, as we shall say,

'open to the World.'" Man is therefore "capable of transforming
the primary centers of resistence and reaction into 'objects.'" For
this reason, then, "spirit is objectivity. . . . More precisely: in order
to be a bearer of spirit, the being must have *reversed*, dynamically
and in principle, its relationship both to external reality and to
itself as compared with the animal, including its intelligence."[45]

This, then, is the difference: a man possesses a center of activity,
a spirit which is "pure actuality" through which his entire surrounding world is raised to the status of "object," liberated from its
"reality" in the sense of a mere nexus of resistance or stimuli.[46]
This is why man is able to understand or, in a sense, "de-realize"
things, enabling them to become objects or "essences" in the phenomenological sense.[47] The human species is not to be measured
by this ability alone, however. Man is able, by virtue of his spiritual
activity, to bring about a second dimension or grade of reflection.
He can "collect" or "concentrate" himself in order to achieve a
special, specific knowledge of his authentic essence. This knowledge of his own spiritual energy is not systematic, because "spirit
is the only being incapable of becoming an object. It is pure actuality." We can nevertheless "'collect' ourselves with regard to our
being as a person: we can concentrate upon it."[48]

The difference between man and all other beings originates in
this *concentration* or unsystematic but prior kind of knowledge. Man
is not simply that creature which has an objective understanding
of the world. He is not merely that being which converts its surroundings into an object, thus freeing himself of strict determinism.
He is in addition the condition of the possibility of converting the
world into objects, the condition of the possibility of all objectivity—of all "objective" experience in general. As a spiritual being,
man is the a priori of all objective knowledge.[49] Thanks to this
"a priori" (the spirit) he has *a different kind* of knowledge: it is not
systematic or objective but rather a form of withdrawal and "identification," a more original and "legitimate" knowledge, if you like,
precisely because it is the ground of the legitimacy of all objective
knowledge.

This notion summarizes and specifies the question of knowledge that precedes objective knowledge, of knowledge that is of a different character from objective knowledge while being at the same time the source and condition of it—the question raised by Fichte. The methodological consequences of this problem are clear. In order to realize this primordial knowledge a different line of inquiry is required quite unlike the usual study of objects. Knowledge of the essence of man must be accompanied by a means of gaining access to man's innermost essence. This method—identification, "comprehension"—will enable us to sneak up on the unconditioned condition of all knowledge without recourse to subterfuge. This very comprehension, withdrawal, or identification is at the root of all reflection on man "as an object"; it is therefore indirectly at the root of all investigations of all objects. By means of this prior inquiry the anhypothetical condition of knowing objects can be explained. The possibility of the existence of objects can be "grounded" and legitimized and the forward advance of science can be assured.

Philosophical anthropology will thus have succeeded in pointing out its true object and acquired the proper set of steps leading to it. It should definitely take advantage of "the vast accumulation of knowledge in the new human sciences." And yet "The increasing multiplicity of the special sciences that deal with man, valuable as they are, tend to hide his nature more than they reveal it."[50] The human sciences have meaning only if they are preceded by an analysis of man's essence, an analysis which demands a different kind of method. By this analysis the steady advance of the human sciences is assured, as not only the "object" of these sciences is at stake but also the epistemological status of all science, which can be safeguarded only if the source of dissemination and the "ground" of all knowledge is found. The human sciences therefore require an anthropology. This anthropology will benefit from the other sciences, but by providing them not with a partial but a whole object of study and guaranteeing that their methodology is legitimate it will be of even more benefit to them. Philosophical anthropology will become the science of the "ultimate ground," assuming all of the prestige of a "first philosophy" and a "basic science." It alone will be able to define the ultimate gound while at the same time identifying the correct goals of investigation in all of the sciences which study "man": the natural sciences and medicine; the sciences of prehistory, ethnology, history and sociology, clinical psychology, evolutionary psychology, and social taxonomy.[51]

The problems raised by the "Copernican Revolution" (as soon as it points out the "human subject") reach their high point and hegemony in Scheler's work. All of the commonplaces associated with these problems are finally, firmly, established. Man is known in his completeness. He is also seen to be the condition of all knowledge, thanks to his essential condition (in his case, a "spiritual" one): he is the genuine unconditioned condition, like the Platonic Good. Unlike the Good, however, he obtains his primordial, prior knowledge from himself. This knowledge is not "objective" in the "scientific" sense: it is knowledge attained "through withdrawal" and identification. Unlike Kant's knowledge of the unity of the *cogitare* of apperception, this knowledge is absolutely sure: it is full, radical knowledge which enables us to discover the spiritual principle that converts all "things" into objects capable of being systematically analyzed. Man is thus the authentic "transcendental subject." He is at the same time an "object," however, to the extent that he can be analyzed by the methods of the other "human sciences." These should nevertheless be preceded by a grounding explanation which reaches to the very heart of its object, that is, man. The human sciences will require anthropology to lead and ground them. This philosophical anthropology will assume the importance of a "first philosophy." It will be a reflection on "grounded elements," and as it investigates the conditions of possibility of all science, it will issue directives to the other sciences. These conditions will be found in man. All science will revolve around man, every "object" will bear the mark of the "human subject's" mediation, which alone allows "objects" to be constituted as such.

Nevertheless, this decisive event at the high point of the anthropological inquiry has its weaknesses. They scarcely rise to the
surface of consciousness, or they are felt as more or less repressed
forebodings. A pause now and then in moments of lucidity gives
them away. Max Scheler is aware that he is taking an active part
in one of those sudden exaltations of human consciousness. Man
is weighted down at the very center of the epistemological configuration. But he asks himself: What does this responsibility, this
exaltation mean? A random—perhaps rhetorical—question is
asked and sooner or later will be heard: What do these exaltations
mean? Are they a process by which man gradually grasps his objective position and his place in the overall scheme of things with
greater depth and accuracy? Or are they milestones in the evolution
of a *dangerous illusion*, symptoms of a more and more serious
disease?[52]

Our present-day generation is now answering this last question
in the affirmative. . . .

3. The Dialectic

Ever since Feuerbach the point of departure has been the same:
the tenet that all knowledge of reality is based on facts. The human
sciences, such as anthropology, starts from facts, not "abstractions"
or "ideas." What matters is constantly to uphold this methodological ideal.

Depending on how this proposition is understood, however, we
may weaken our methodology.

When the ideal of scientific knowledge is applied to nature it
simply furthers the progress of science. But when applied to
society it turns out to be an ideological weapon of the
bourgeoisie.[53]

All facts therefore appear to be imprisoned by the way in which
they are interpreted. In order to study facts, empiricism must make

use of "abstraction," reducing natural facts to observable phenomena which evidence regularity. But can this approach of the natural sciences—an approach which assures their evolution—be extrapolated to the domain of man? Is it legitimate to use methods of abstraction and reduction in a realm in which all "facts" are mixed together into a "whole"?[54] Lukács' answer leaves no room for doubt. The sociohistorical totality of man cannot be factionalized or reduced to abstractions. All inquiries must have the "whole" actively in mind, even if the object of study is limited to a specific phenomenon like a historical period or a type of social behavior. Otherwise the very nature of the thing being studied is lost, and with it the very meaning of human history.

This is why the abstract method is not "scientific" when it comes to man. It tends to break apart what is in fact a unitary process (human history).[55] No specialized study can afford to lose sight of this overall process.[56] The abstract method should therefore be replaced by a method whose object is the totality of human history, and the method which investigates the "actual whole" is dialectics.

The object of dialectics, however, is not the cut-and-dried investigation of the evolution of a unitary, objective process. With Engels, the proper domain of dialectics is held to be the confrontation of "subject" and "object," the investigation of contradictions and the supposed unity of these two terms, the woof and warp of human evolution.[57]

The specific nature of the domain in question is based on this as well as on its need for a method which differs from the method appropriate to the "natural" domain. To study the dialectic is not simply to study an "object" or an "objective process." When we study a society at a specific stage of its evolution we are also studying the "form of consciousness" that corresponds to that stage. Forms of subjectivity appear alongside the objective processes and are intertwined with them. Dialectics does not study each aspect separately. On the contrary, it studies the necessary connection between the two. It studies the "dialectic" of the subject and the object.

To investigate only the "objective processes" means therefore to "abstract" the subject-object totality and undermine the very domain under investigation. It means to block the road to understanding. All "abstractions" must therefore be rejected—all "scientificist" studies which eliminate the "subjective" dimension and all "idealist" studies which limit themselves to "forms of consciousness." The "abstract method" leads to two deviations: it eliminates subjectivity by reifying it, studying man, his relationships, and kind of consciousness as if they were "things"; and it eliminates "objective processes," viewing them as the product of subjectivity and consciousness. If one uses the abstract method one must choose one or the other. Both undermine the domain of human history, which can only be studied when the subjective and objective aspects are held present and analyzed in terms of the tension between them at each stage of history.[58]

The fact is that man is not merely a "form of consciousness," as idealism would have it, nor a "thing" as "revisionist (scientificist) literature" claims. Yet under specific historical conditions man can appear before consciousness in this or that form, and this suggests the study of these pathological ways in which man comes into self-consciousness. These types of "false consciousness" or "ideological" modes of man's knowledge of himself and his relationships should be studied in connection with the "objective processes" that make these forms of consciousness possible. The dialectic should begin, like Feuerbach and Marx's anthropology, with an "expurgatione," an investigation of ideologies that is not limited to "refuting" these deceitful representations but rather studies—dialectically—the necessity of those "false consciousnesses" corresponding to specific forms taken by objective processes in the eyes of consciousness.[59] In this manner we can understand why under certain historical conditions the very products of human work can appear to the consciousness as "independent things" which have "social relationships" among themselves, hiding the human reality that makes possible both the work and the relationships.[60]

The dialectic must shatter these deceitful representations or fetishes created by the "appearance of reality." It must shatter this appearance itself, this "false totality" in order to penetrate to the very essence of man's social reality, in order to understand the nature of those products (merchandise) which by their very nature veil their own essence and reality as products of *human* labor.[61]

This correct, dialectical kind of knowledge cannot come about, however, by sharpening the judgment or eliminating "idols" by the exercise of a keener understanding. The right conditions must prevail for the right kind of knowledge to be created. The knowing "subject" must in the end find himself in a position to understand the very essence of "objective" social and historical processes because of his "situation." Human subjectivity must find itself in the proper circumstances in order to understand its own reality.[62] This circumstance or situation becomes clear only when a "class" appears whose vocation is to eliminate all classes and divisions within mankind, when a social class is called on to put an end to man's fragmentation into classes, identifying itself at last with "Humanity" as a whole and reappropriating the alienated essence of man. This class, the proletariat, is by virtue of its own objective situation the class which stands on the threshold of knowing man's essence as a social being and of understanding history as a comprehensible, unitary process. To the extent that it is the one class called upon to suppress all classes, the proletariat is by virtue of its own objective situation led to the threshold of correct knowledge of man's social reality. Its consciousness corresponds to that essence. In it the subjective and the objective elements coincide. At last theory becomes praxis. Knowledge is immediately transformed into revolution. The proletariat is thus the vocation of Humanity: in it are eliminated all of the scissions that break man's completeness apart: theory and praxis, consciousness and being, subject and object, etc. Dialectics is thus the method corresponding to the proletariat.[63]

This approach is everywhere visible in the post-Kantian epistemological configuration, even though it is only one possible (definitely not necessary) answer. What matters is that the problems are quite clear: "human facts" cannot be known if man's essence is not known. The latter is not simply a "thing," an "object," but rather the unity of "subject and object." Every method which falsely abstracts one of these elements from the whole must be eliminated. In exchange, a method must be developed which studies man in his completeness. Man is not merely a fact of nature: he is also the "consciousness" of all "facts of nature" and as such should be studied without one or the other of these elements being singled out. To the study of the elemental aspect of human subjectivity, the object of philosophical anthropology; and to the study of man's creations (products of his labor), the object of the human sciences—to these dialectics adds the study of both factors, focusing on the changes and evolution that they undergo. Dialectics studies the relationships and mobility of both terms at the heart of a totality which is never broken apart, although under special conditions it might occasionally *appear* to be fragmented. Dialectics studies evolution or human history: the objective forms created by man in his work and his creative praxis. It studies the types of consciousness that correspond to this praxis.

4. The Human Sciences

There can be no question that the task of the human sciences is to chart man's creations in all of their universal forms, to study human creativity in its entire magnitude—in the kind of association and community that characterize it, in its economic productivity, cultural works, and so forth. The human sciences must likewise study the social and cultural systems created by man in the course of his history: systems of consolidating or exchanging goods, systems of meaning and communication, all kinds of symbolic systems. The human sciences must study human behavior in its concrete forms—that is, they should study man on the basis of his works. They will regard men "as if they were facts," social, cultural, and spiritual facts that can be approached like any natural process and with the same analytical methods.[64] But from the "external" examination of the human object the human sciences should infer an "internal" a priori which makes externality and objectivity possible. They must constantly infer a dimension of man that cannot be reduced to any "objectification," because it is the condition of all objectification. The human sciences will thus require a philosophy of man which makes this objectification possible, investigating man's essence, his specific, generic activity, understood as the creation of his own means of survival, consolidation, exchange, and symbolization. This presupposes an "anthropology" that systematizes man's essence and creative activity or praxis, the foundation of all objective production. This need will be reinforced by the fact that the study of this original essence enables us to systematize the very condition of knowledge and understanding, as man is both the subject and the object of his own inquiry and analysis, both subject and object of knowledge. And to the extent that man is the subject, he requires a previous clarification of all "objective" analysis.

The human sciences thus demand a philosophy of man. Without it they cannot legitimate their epistemological status. They must rest on a firm epistemological foundation if they are to be sciences, if they are to gather knowledge. This foundation can only be laid if the condition of possibility of all knowledge is understood, and this is man in his role as the condition of objectivity. This inquiry also requires a different means of approach than the human sciences. It cannot make use of their characteristically analytical methodology. Rather, it demands a "comprehensive" method which takes all of human nature "into account," making possible and even endorsing an "analysis."[65]

Of course the sociologist must study social facts "as if they were things," viewing them "from without."[66] Goldmann, however, asks if this methodological ideal is "epistemologically possible."[67] It is possible in part, but only if it follows an investigation of man "from without," as "man" (not thing) and as "subject" (not merely object). The human sciences require that this inquiry be epistemologically grounded, because the "fact of man"—the starting point of all investigations—is only comprehensible if one realizes that man, being "object" at the same time he is "subject," is a substance external to the investigator and somehow the investigator's accomplice—that, insofar as he is "man," he is inextricably bound up in the investigation. Man is clearly the sum of everything he creates, the result of his activity and his praxis. And this activity refers back to a primordial, constitutive subject whose essence and meaning must be clarified by a philosophy of man and whose mobility—the evolution from agent to act—must be studied by a "dialectic."

Every investigation in the field of the human sciences must therefore be preceded in a quite monotonous way by apparently rhetorical admonishments which are in fact inseparable from the problems being described. In the study of languages we will be told not to forget that language is first and foremost an invention of Man. In sociological studies we will be told that the social relationships under analysis are *human* creations, and in studies of cultural products we will be told that the norms, values, and patterns evidenced by these products are the creations of men—that the artifacts, tools, and symbolic systems are all created by Man. In the process, more than a simple tautology is affirmed and more is said than what is already assumed: we are reminded that the study of Man as the condition of creation of "human works" must precede and provide the basis for the study of these works, rather than being separated from them. With these superficially vacuous exhortations, which only seem tautological if one lives immersed in these problems, comes the implicit comment that all investigations in the domain of the "human sciences" must be preceded by a clarification of man's essence and basic structure—that is, an "anthropology" or "philosophy of man."

With this, the configuration opened up by Kantian critical philosophy, which took concrete form in "idealism" and in Feuerbach's anthropology, declares that all of its possibilities have been exhausted. The rest is repetition, monotony, a burdensome surplus of commonplaces. The two terms of this configuration—the transcendent human subject and the "object"—have given of themselves everything they had to give. They have made possible the systematic study of the human subject (anthropology), the systematic study of the object constituted by this subject (the human sciences which study human "works"), the systematic study of the dialectic of subject and object which offers a dynamic picture of the whole of human existence in the tension and movement (history) obtaining between these terms. Even the "natural sciences" somehow require the "human sciences"—anthropology and dialectics—to the extent that natural processes become "objects" of knowledge, thus referring back to conditions of objectivity comprehensible only in terms of the subject or transcendental self-consciousness. This epistemological configuration thus presents itself as a many-pointed star; it extends and retracts its points in a double motion of throwing off and gathering in, the double motion of the transcendental human Subject and the Unconditioned that belongs to the configuration.

A wealth of consequences follows on this. They can be tracked down one by one in the reflections of post-Kantian thought. One can follow the ontological consequences, for instance. The human Subject will always be the root, the unconditioned condition. Without it no knowledge is possible. Without it reality is split into two vast domains—the domain of subjectivity, of man and spirit, and the domain of "objectivity," of the outer world, of nature and of things. Nature will be understood as either the "externalization of Mind" (Hegel), the "power from without" which human practice is called upon to "humanize" (Marx) or that which exists "in itself," which human nature is called upon to "de-totalize" or "a-nihil-ate" (Sartre). Methodological consequences: two means of study, two "sciences" correspond to the realm of "being"—the natural sciences and the sciences of the spirit (the sciences of man or "culture"). All of the problems raised will attempt to structure the methods corresponding to each of these vast disciplines. Dilthey and the "Neokantians" are stark testimony to these concerns. Finally, what are the "theological" consequences? Man will be elevated to the rank of the one and only God, the foundation of all morality and political, literary, aesthetic, and social activity. The various "currents of thought" called "humanist" will then challenge this Deity. Once the idols of yesteryear have been proclaimed, existentialism, Marxism, and the confessional philosophies will elect Man to be the true God. Several varieties of humanist Marxism and "radical theology" will announce similar proposals to foment the reign of God-Mankind on earth, in this way laying the basis for a "dialogue."

PART III: TWILIGHT

1. Holzwege

In *Being and Time* the inquiry into the "meaning of being" followed the well-traveled tracks of the problems we have been discussing. A clarification of the question about Being should precede any clarification of the meaning of Being, and an analysis of the questioning entity should come first of all. The analysis of Dasein must come before any ontological investigation.[68]

Apparently nothing has changed but the ways of expressing *the same thing*. But something has happened nevertheless. Man is still at the center of the plot, it seems, the privileged object of investigation. But in order to manifest his own structure he has had to disappear. He has foundered on the very a priori structure that makes him possible. "Being-in-the-world" is no longer a subject of anthropology, as Heidegger admits. The analytical procedure regarding Dasein cannot be mistaken for a kind of anthropology. Being-in-the-world is the a priori of this subject in the same way that the analytical procedure is "prior" to anthropology.[69] Heidegger clearly has not broken with the problems introduced by Kantianism: he has only exacerbated them. Far from moving away from them, he attempts to rethink them from the ground up, giving them a radical new interpretation while never straying from the foundation. He attempts to think about this configuration in a primordially new way. It is an impossible task: Heidegger has tried to say something *different* by immersing himself in what has remained *the same*. His attempt signals the twilight of a configuration which finally closes in on itself and slowly disappears.

Being and Time initiates a progressively more profound inquiry which culminates in *Unterwegs zur Sprache*. There is a continuity between these works which cannot be disproven by critics who put their trust in appearances.[70] The inquiry in *Being and Time* is directed toward an a priori structure which constitutes the condition of possibility of the "classical" subject of anthropology. Little by little, the investigation becomes more radical, more hectic, pointing toward the structure which makes Dasein possible. The Temporality of Dasein refers back to a more fundamental, earlier Temporality: the Temporality of Being.

All other traces of "subjectivism" are apparently eliminated from *Being and Time*. Dasein does not play the role of a transcendental entity without referring back to an unconditioned condition other than itself. Instead of being centered in Dasein, the unconditioned condition now tends to establish itself in a kind of "Being" which is the Transcendent of transcendence, the unconditioned condition of Dasein. This Being nevertheless requires the presence of Dasein as its means of opening itself, as its neighbor and its shepherd. Man will certainly no longer be the one who speaks and thinks: it is rather Being which manifests itself through man, in his thought and his song. It is Language that speaks and Thought that thinks, through the poet and the philosopher. And this original language and thought are born of and develop from the unconditioned condition entity which is Being.[71]

By requiring the presence of Dasein, however, this Being finds itself caught in the circuit of subjectivity and "anthropology." In some sense it is the hypostasis of the subject, a hypostasis that the subject, in order to found and legitimize itself, constantly challenges. A subject that no longer desires to be a subject. Man is thus the desubjectivized subject who finally attempts to abolish the slavery imposed on him by the transcendental horizon which is trapped in subjectivity and anthropology. Heidegger makes a lucid attempt to "distance" the transcendental level from the subjective realm of man. But even while he challenges it, he himself remains trapped in the same realm. He restricts his enterprise to inverting the relationship of conditioner and conditioned, elaborating the hypothesis that Man is the unconditioned condition, is Being.

Heidegger does not break with the configuration because he welcomes "man" into his philosophy, if only as a neighbor or shepherd of being. He does not break with "humanism," "anthropology," or "subjectivism." He does, however, specify the final path, the "lost path," the "cul de sac" of the configuration. After Heidegger this configuration can only be traversed as a monotonous, deathlike repetition of something utterly familiar. Heidegger's "lost path" (*Holzwege*) does not lead anywhere at all.[72]

But this same "nowhere" is both an excess of light, in respect to its own configuration, and an opening up of new horizons of reflection. The path that leads to Being is wayward: Being is nowhere to be found, it either does not appear at all or appears in its hiddenness alone. Being is always "beyond." Heidegger's progressive inquiry into into the human a priori and the a priori of this a priori, his attempt to investigate a Transcendental Transcendent, ends in an infinite regress. The goal is unreachable, and this unreachable thing is Being. To the extent that "man" is still inextricably entwined with his own philosophy, he cannot be gotten rid of without his reappearing as his own hypostasis or inversion. To the extent that we want to free ourselves of both, a Transcendent pops up in the form of a "non-appearance," a Transcendental Transcendent that is always beyond, always postulated by a human subject who "knows" it in the way that it does not know it at all, as it is trapped in anthropological structures from the moment it appears to man. Heidegger knows that in this way Being becomes a prisoner: he therefore proposes another kind of "opening" in which Being appropriates these structures to itself, opening itself to being understood by man. The suspicion that this may be a mere inversion or hypostasis of "what is already familiar," however, indicates the sheer impossibility of the task.

This Being from beyond thus promotes a trajectory similar to that of the Platonic Good. The only means of approach is no longer cognitive but rather "mystical." Being can only be known in its unknowability, can only be discovered in its concealment. Being lies beyond. Nothing can be known of it now except as a kind of non-knowing, that is, in the present context, as a kind of nihilization of the human subject, in man's liberation from himself and from his "kinds" of knowledge—in his simple availability or openness to a kind of knowing that can no longer "reach" him or that has already strayed from the course by the time it reaches him.

Heidegger thus brings to a close an epistemological configuration which allows neither transcendence nor groundings that are alien to the "anthropological subject." The way he opens leads nowhere in the sense that it proposes to open a road that goes in the opposite direction without first liquidating the "anthropological subject." The epistemological configuration has its requirements, though, and Heidegger's path is thus closed to traffic. It nevertheless indicates, albeit somewhat blindly, a different realm of reflection, a new configuration. This new realm will restructure the totality of pertinent epistemological elements, however, some of which, like the human subject in its capacity of unconditioned condition, are slowly effaced from memory. Another unconditioned condition, other elements, and a new structure will take their place. Man will be erased from the horizon, his "divine" prestige will gradually diminish. The twilight of man-as-God now begins.

2. Toward a New Configuration

It seems the question is always the same: What is man? Marx's criticism of Feuerbach is simply another answer to the same problem:

> Feuerbach resolves the essence of religion into the essence of *man*. But the essence of man is no abstraction inherent to each individual. In its reality it is the *ensemble* (aggregate) of social relations.[73]

We are moving in clearly humanist territory: "the essence of man is no abstraction," *but rather*. . . . Philosophy's task is once again to define man's being. Making full use of the commonplaces associated with inquiries that necessarily begin by eliminating all the "misleading ideas" and "pseudorepresentations" that man forms about himself—that is, all "abstractions"—Marx once again begins with an *expurgatione* designed to lead ultimately to the true, concrete being of man. Because in effect, "the essence of man. . . . in its reality (*in seiner Wirklichkeit*) is . . . ."

What does the answer matter? The very questions asked and problems posed condition it in such a way that question and answer remain hopelessly entangled. This is irrefutable unless the answer is in complete disharmony with the question—that is, unless the proposed definition of man is no longer a definition at all.

"In its reality it (the essence of man) is the *ensemble* (aggregate) of social relations (*das ensemble der gesellschaftlichen Verhältnisse*)." A disconcerting answer: an unbridgeable abyss separates the definition from what is defined. "The essence of man is . . . ." This statement points inexorably toward human essence and existence, toward that trait or set of traits which uniquely characterize man in relation to other entities. The statement persistently follows the path originally traveled by Feuerbach, much later by Max Scheler and Heidegger. Man is "a being to whom his species, his essential nature, is an object of thought." Man is the one being who is able, because of his spiritual dimension, to convert reality into objective form. As Sartre says, man is that being who stands on the threshold of "nihilizing" being-in-itself, because man in any strict sense does not "exist" but rather *makes* his being by freely projecting himself. Man, the shepherd and neighbor of Being, is the entity in which Being makes itself known. In all of these answers one already knows or assumes beforehand that man has the prerogative to boast of his status as the unconditioned condition of all knowledge, which he has by virtue of his very essence and existence. Without man there is no knowing. Without man understanding, eidetic intuition, the grasping of meaning—all of these are impossible. Man presupposes a transcendental consciousness: he is basically the "transcendental subject." The process of clarifying his being takes us sooner or later to the safe harbor in which all post-Kantian reflection is communicated, generating "mutual understanding."

Marx's answer veers off in an unexpected direction, however. When we define man as "the ensemble of social relations," it is as if we were weighing his essence against the outcome of his "essential activity." It would appear that Marx has slipped. He should say: "Man is a being whose generic activity is social labor and praxis, and by virtue of this labor and praxis he establishes a totality of social relations." The "structure" (of society) must necessarily result from a primordial activity which makes it possible. Marx's definition is nonessential: in discussing the consequence he ignores the cause. He gives a metonymic answer to the question. His statement should be changed to read: "man *creates* the totality of social relations."

We can nevertheless identify a "slip" in another sense—a slip not in the definition but in what is supposedly being defined. In fact the definition does not define "man." The term "man" is superfluous. Marx's statement presupposes the basic point of the "Manuscripts," namely, that man is the root, the starting point of all reflection. But this assumption has now been transformed: "The root, the starting point, is the totality of social relations." In fact this statement should be revised to read: given the original equation of man = root, we here calculate that social relations = root. But Marx, absorbed in his debate with Feuerbach, halfway between the anthropological problems and the problems that he was to outline in this and later works, now substitutes man's "equal" (root) for "man." Only by now it is no longer his equal, or it is so only in the form of a hesitancy, a slip, an abortive act. The old problems are still in full force: they still exact their last-minute demands. But now the notion of man is gradually seen to be superfluous. It has to be put "in quotes," in the same way that the set of notions implied by "man"—like *Entfremdung*—is put in quotes and used to ironic effect in *The German Ideology*.

The starting point of all inquiries, the initial datum, the "fact" on which all science now flourishes is "the ensemble of social relations." The individual disappears, despite the fact that Marx suddenly breaks into *The German Ideology* as if to sing his swan song. Neither the empirical individual nor the "abstract individual" (hypostasis of the other) has the status of a "starting point" any longer. It is not the individual—not the essence or substance of each individual—but the "relationship" that matters now. Attention shifts from the dense substance of man, be it "in motion" or at rest, toward the "social relation." A new set of problems is thus introduced in which the structure of this ensemble of relations and the structural conditions of possibility of any given relationship must be studied. "Man," the "individual," the "human person," all disappear. Other concepts take their place in the theory which deals with the problems raised by Marx, concepts like group, class, structure, etc. Marx opens up a field in which sociology is at last possible—that is, a science which studies the essence of society not by referring to the "human condition" that makes it possible but rather by treating society as an ensemble of social relations. Guided by this first datum it then moves toward the "structure" that makes possible these "factual relationships" which at first seem to be the most basic datum.

This shift in the point of departure automatically shifts the terms of the epistemological configuration. This is clear in *The German Ideology* and continues to characterize the works of Marx's later years.

"Life is not determined by consciousness, but consciousness by life."[74] In its context this statement cannot be mistaken for a mere "inversion" of Hegel's idealist scheme, even though its polemical nature might lead one to that conclusion. Once again, the problem appears to be "traditional." The answer is framed in different terms than the question, however. The claim that "life" (social being) determines consciousness assumes the definition of social reality as the "ensemble of social relations" that comprises a "structure." This statement means that (human) consciousness or self-consciousness can no longer attain the status of unconditioned condition of knowledge, let alone of "reality," as it does in idealism. This would-be consciousness founders on those very conditions of possibility that make it—precariously—possible. In fact, consciousness breaks apart into unconsciousness, into the specific forms of consciousness and the specific relations that correspond to each stage of creative power. The "forms of consciousness" find themselves subject to a kind of determinism that is imposed on them, a "structure" into which they are built and from which they cannot escape. There is consequently a lack of equilibrium between what men think about themselves and their true relationships, between what men "want," "desire," or "fancy" and what their relationships really are. Human knowledge and "practice" find themselves subject to the tyranny of a preconditioning structure—the unconscious structure of thought or ideology, which determines what men think, and the hidden structure of society, which determines what men do. The old human Deity, that completeness laboriously pieced together in the wake of Kant, that synthesis of human parts (theoretical reason, praxis, emotion) cedes to an anonymous structure, the new unconditioned condition of knowledge. In it are resolved the enigmas and fetishes that *appear* in man's sight, weaving the very fabric of his consciousness—a consciousness which is in fact unconsciousness.

Of course one can read Marx, as Lukács does, making use of the received ideas of Hegelianism. This "(class) unconsciousness" can be conceived of as a "relative consciousness" or a "not-yet-consciousness" that points toward the eventual Victory and Celebration of a kind of Self-Consciousness that finally knows its own essence (spiritual essence in Hegel, "human and material" essence in Lukács—the difference is one of nuance). Hegelian-type eschatology is not totally eradicated from the problems Marx addressed in his later years. In addition, he failed to develop the "theory of ideology" hinted at in *The German Ideology* and scattered throughout his other works. He failed to develop those concepts which find their way into his works as "unconsciousness." This is why "historical laws" can be understood independently from consciousness and will, in the Hegelian sense that men unwittingly carry out a providential plan that uses its instruments quite *shrewdly*. Another reading is possible, however, in which the whole Hegelian eschatology, the entire teleology of the "as-yet-unconscious" consciousness that becomes the self-consciousness of the human spirit in and for itself through protracted "labor," no longer has a place. Hegel begins with absolute knowledge, that is, the self-consciousness of the spirit or subject which has reentered the realm of matter. But in Marx these notions of "self-consciousness" and "subject" no longer play the same relevant role as they did in Hegel. Knowledge, like all human activity, derives from an unconscious structure that subjugates it to its own rules and conditions. Knowledge no longer becomes legitimate with a *self-knowledge* that refers back to some subject's reflections. Knowing refers to an anonymous *Self* which establishes a set of cognitive rules by means of which things can be approached.

3. The Unconscious as "Unconditioned"

The new configuration thus described offers only two new terms. The starting point is "empirical," if you wish: a group of social relations or institutions, "sentences," a "discourse" or group of texts, etc. But from this initial datum we must work back to the "field" in which the datum is made intelligible, that is, to its condition of possibility. If this is to happen the datum cannot be isolated from a group of data with which it has, or is thought to have, a systematic relationship. The underlying structure of these relationships, which makes them possible and directs them—the structure that distributes the constitutive elements and organizes the whole—must be *conceived*. Now, this structure is "hidden," "latent," unconscious. The structure that makes possible our "speech," our "sentences," our "discourses," our activities of exchange and association, our behavior—this structure is "invisible." It does not appear on the "empirical" level, nor can it be "seen" or "read," no matter how incisive our scrutiny.

The unconscious underlying structure is also the unconditioned condition of all knowledge. Critical activity is no longer concerned with a "transcendental subject" but rather with a "transcendental unconsciousness." The a priori form of thought and the condition of our knowledge are no longer legitimated by the unity of perception but by the unconscious structure that rules our speaking, our acting, our perceptions, knowledge, and science. The scientific task par excellence is to explore these structures. All of the social sciences—linguistics after Saussure and Sapir, ethnology after Boas, psychology beginning with Freud, sociology beginning with

Marx—all tend to isolate *invisible structures* underlying *what is visible*. Chomsky finds the hidden structure of language, Lévi-Strauss the structure of the "unconscious mind" whose modus vivendi can be inferred from social institutions and myth, Foucault the unconscious structure of knowledge, etc. The duality of what is hidden and what is revaled identifies the two terms of this new configuration: what is hidden is the condition of what is revealed. It is also the unconditioned, as it refers back to nothing other than itself. It belongs to the order of the unconscious, the systematized, structural order which makes possible what is revealed. The "systems" of language, society and culture, myth and science (episteme) are the respective conditions of "speech," of social and cultural institutions, of myths and of the sciences. These two relevant terms turn up over and over again in all of the disciplines that take shape within this configuration. Their mutual, sustaining relationship indicates the specificity of a configuration which breaks with all those we have previously described.

This configuration provides no place for man and his attributes. It transfers his aggregating function to the anonymous ranks of "system." On the basis of these premises a process can be described which has yet to be begun, a process which should rightly be completed by a "critique," in the Kantian sense, of the "science" of our time. This critique can no longer have the goal of identifying a unifying, transcendental subject that is the basis of all experience but rather a "transcendental unconscious" provided with a priori categories and forms that make experience possible.

This "constructive" task must nevertheless be preceded by an "expurgation." Or, to state this more cautiously, the "limits" of our problems regarding knowledge and philosophy must first be established, as well as the boundaries which enclose other sets of problems like those we have been describing and *turn them in upon themselves*. To recall them enables us better to situate ourselves and to keep them present as points of reference.

There is no doubt about the conclusion drawn from this *anam-*

nesis: that our present philosophy also leaves no room for man. We can no longer perpetuate the old idyll of anthropology and philosophy. Our current philosophy is not so much a "philosophy of the death of man," as Garaudy claims, as a philosophy which marks the "death of the philosophy of man."

As always, Hegel's assertion is substantiated once again: philosophy, too, arrives too late at the funeral, too late at the mass. Since Marx, the social sciences have eliminated "man" as a relevant theoretical concept. For some time now literature has been a lament for the absence of new dimensions:

> The exclusive cult of the "human" has given way to a larger consciousness, one that is less anthropocentric. The novel seems to stagger, having lost what was once its best prop, the hero. If it does not manage to right itself, it is because its life was linked to that of a society now past. If it does manage, on the contrary, a new course lies open to it, with the promise of new discoveries.[75]

For some time now we have been reading novels in which the subject, the "I," no longer plays a dominant role. This probably dates from that day when the "subject" who introduces the story of *The Murder of Roger Ackroyd* began to vacillate. We can still recall that day with some horror and awe: suddenly, the narrator started losing his composure. All of our expectations came tumbling down. We began to suspect the "subject" when Hercule Poirot failed to converse with him in his customary way. He kept an ironic distance, was full of reticence toward the doctor-narrator. And little by little this "subject" weakened: his discourse became more and more careless and disorganized. Poirot peppered him with questions. Yes, we became *suspicious* of this "I," and in the end we found a culprit with no alibi. There was only one course of action left to this condemned "I": to leave the story to posterity in a manuscript and next to it his own corpse. The "I" dies with the manuscript by his own hand, swallowing Veronal. With his death a new dimension of literature is opened up, a hidden territory that had lain in shadow when his presence was still felt.

Narrative technique has gotten rid of that bothersome presence in the process. It sacrificed the protagonist in the same way criticism sacrificed the "author." We all know about this and we have all been spreading the word: the moment has arrived, then, for philosophy, the redundant activity par excellence, to make the same pronouncement—without fanfare but with a touch of melancholy in the gathering darkness.

4. Subjectivity Adrift

Some philosophies tend to applaud this "death of man" as if it meant the death of an "antiquated idea" of man and heralded the rebirth of a "new man." On the other hand, this is the exegesis opened up by Nietzsche's proclamation that the "last man" had died and the *Übermensch* had arrived on the scene. The latter, Man with a capital M, confronts the deceitful image that man has fashioned for himself in the bosom of "Western culture." He heralds a new, more critical, more solid notion of man to be developed in the future. A less frail and less ingenuous philosophy of man, a "new humanism."

But let us abandon these pious and slightly boring proclamations and attend a more appealing, albeit somewhat cruel spectacle. Its drawing card is the reappearance of character long since retired from the stage: the clown is making his comeback.

The years have not passed for naught, though: this powerful, fear-inspiring subject, who ruled the reader in every detail—the main character, omniscient and supremely glib—has returned a broken, spiritually impoverished and, what is worse, stupid individual. With every step he takes in the outskirts of Hong Kong he loses his bearings, his memory, and his balance. He is constantly going blank, forgetting things, getting muddled, and contradicting himself. He doesn't know anything at all any more.

La maison de rendez-vous is such a cruel experiment! The "subject" has been allowed back on stage at last. It is his turn to speak, but for a short time only. Besides, he is always getting lost: "In parks,

Philosophy Without Man

I organize celebrations."[76] No doubt that Lady Ava, the mistress of the house, is speaking. No doubt? "I approach the mistress of the house in my turn and bow, while she holds out her long fingers whose nails are a little too red."[77] This "first person" is always shifting from one person to the next, as if it were a "third person." It has no unity.

This "I" no longer guides the reader. It is no longer the very condition of possibility of the story, that which confers unity. On the contrary, it is as lost and bewildered as the reader. Its function is inverted: now it leads the reader into anxious bewilderment. It is a subject who *knows virtually nothing*. He builds his hypotheses on what has happened and then attempts to verify or discard them:

> But one thing disturbs me now: wouldn't the lieutenant actually be walking toward the mistress of the house in that resolute way of his? Isn't it more logical to arrest her, in the first place? As a matter of fact, Lady Ava hasn't made any secret, during a conversation with Kim—during a monologue, more exactly (for there is no point playing with words) . . .[78]

This recurrent first person no longer has anything to do, at bottom, with the traditional subject. It is a shiftless subject who goes astray, changes places: from one displacement to the next it carries over in the anonymous unity of a mere "pronoun." It has been integrated into a different system, one which blocks any complicity with the first person of traditional narrative. And yet in its very bewilderment and anguish it makes us think of a Human Subject who was once a wise and powerful monarch. He has been retired for some time now, and with his crown he is slowly losing his head.

Conclusion

The model we built has enabled us both to identify the manner in which the "unconditioned condition" shifts from place to place and to plot some of the possible directions taken by these displacements. The final configuration investigated above showed us the emergence of this mobile term on the "outside" of the knower-knowable duality, an "outside" different from and in some sense the inverse of Plato's. The outside of the "underlying structure" is not *transcendence*. It is not an unconditioned transcendent but an *underlying* one.

Only one slot has remained empty, the slot corresponding to the "unconditioned" adherence to the "knowable." Before declaring it "uninhabitable," however, we should review the history of philosophy. We might find that the slot is filled by those philosophies which interpret the "archetypal idea" as an unconditioned condition—philosophies of a Platonic cast, that is, opposed to the "transcendent" aspect of the Good expressly stated by Plato in the *Republic*.

In any case, our inquiry has achieved its goal of indicating that *configuration* in which "man" has the status of "unconditioned condition," thus enabling philosophy and anthropology to collaborate. Our present-day philosophy leaves no room for this complicity: it still defines itself negatively, as a *philosophy without man*.

Notes

1. Philosophy and Its Shadow

1. These conclusions are reached in G. Dumézil's *Les Dieux indoeuropéens* and *Mythe et Épopée* as well as in Claude Lévi-Strauss's "mythologies," e.g. the "Overture" to *The Raw and the Cooked*.

2. Ernst Cassirer, *The Problem of Knowledge* (New Haven: Yale University Press, 1950) and Joseph Maréchal, *Le point de depart de la métaphysique* (Paris: Alcan, 1927).

3. Edmund Leach, *Rethinking Anthropology* (London: London School of Economics, 1968), Introduction.

4. We might also use the term "filtering." The word "abstraction" unfortunately presupposes a theory of knowledge to which we of course do not subscribe.

5. Leach, *Rethinking Anthropology*.

6. Claude Lévi-Strauss, *Anthropologie Structurale* (Paris: Plon, 1958).

2. The Structure and Function of Philosophy

1. Karl Popper, *The Logic of Scientific Discovery* (New York: Basic Books, 1959).

2. Rudolf Carnap, *The Logical Structure of the World* (Berkeley: University of California Press, 1967).

3. Claude Lévi-Strauss, *The Raw and the Cooked* (New York: Harper Torchbooks, 1970), pp. 35–65.

4. Popper, *The Logic of Scientific Discovery*.

5. See the *Sophist*, 216a et seq., and the *Phaedrus*, 265d et seq.

6. René Descartes, *Rules for the Guidance of our Mental Powers*, in *Philosophical Writings* (London: Macmillan, 1952), p. 8.

7. Immanuel Kant, *Critique of Pure Reason* (New York: Modern Library, 1958), Introduction.

8. Johann Gottlieb Fichte, *Science of Knowledge (Wissenschaftslehre) with the First and Second Introduction* (New York: Appleton-Century-Crofts, 1970).

9. G. W. F. Hegel, *The Phenomenology of Mind* (New York: Harper Torchbooks, 1967).

10. In chapter 7 we will nevertheless see that some philosophers were "relatively conscious" of what they were doing.

11. José Ortega y Gasset, *Ideas y creencias* (Madrid: Revista de Occidente, 1942), p. 20 et seq.

12. Popper, *The Logic of Scientific Discovery*.

13. Michel Foucault, *The Birth of the Clinic* (New York: Pantheon, 1973).

14. I have spoken of this in my book *Filosofía y carnaval* (Barcelona: Anagrama, 1969).

15. Friedrich Nietzsche, *The Will to Power* (New York: Vintage, 1968), Book II, section 3: Critique of Philosophy.

16. G. W. F. Hegel, *Philosophy of Right* (Oxford: Clarendon Press, 1942), p. 13.

17. Michel Foucault, *The Order of Things* (New York: Vintage, 1973). p. 307.

18. Carnap, *The Logical Structure of the World.*

19. Francis Macdonald Cornford, *The Theaetetus and the Sophist of Plato* (London: Routledge and Kegan Paul, 1964).

20. This, briefly, is the "argument" of Lévi-Strauss's *The Elementary Structure of Kinship* (Boston: Beacon Press, 1969).

21. Marcel Mauss, *Oeuvres* (1906), I: Introduction à l'analyse de quelques phénomènes religieux.

22. Lévi-Strauss, *The Elementary Structure of Kinship*, p. 24.

23. Louis Althusser and Etienne Balibar, *Reading Capital* (London: NLB, 1970), p. 26.

24. Foucault, *The Order of Things*, p. 145.

25. M. Amiot, "Le relativisme culturaliste de Michel Foucault," in *Les Temps Modernes*, no. 248 (January 1967).

26. Jean Piaget, *Structuralism* (New York: Basic Books, 1970).

27. Jean Pouillon, "L'oeuvre de Claude Lévi-Strauss," in *Les Temps Modernes*, no. 126 (July 1956), p. 158.

28. Pedro Luis Font, in *Convivium*, no. 24–25, p. 165.

29. Michel Foucault, *Madness and Civilization* (New York: Vintage, 1973), pp. ix–xiii.

30. Michel Foucault, *Maladie mentale et psychologie* (Paris: Presses Universitaires Françaises, 1963), p. 93.

31. G. E. von Grunebaum and R. Caillois, eds., *The Dream and Human Societies* (Berkeley and Los Angeles: University of California Press, 1966).

32. Claude Lévi-Strauss, "Introduction á l'oeuvre de M. Mauss," in Marcel Mauss, *Sociologie et anthropologie* (Paris: Presses Universitaires Françaises, 1968).

33. Mauss, *Sociologie et anthropologie.*

3. Philosophy Without Man

1. Foucault, *The Order of Things* (New York: Vintage, 1973), p. 386.
2. Foucault calls the "ordered space" in terms of which sciences defines itself the "epistemological field" or "episteme."
3. Foucault, *The Order of Things*, p. 373 et seq.
4. See Louis Althusser, *For Marx* (New York: Phantheon, 1969), especially the section on Marxism and humanism, and Claude Lévi-Strauss, *The Savage Mind* (Chicago: University of Chicago Press, 1966).
5. See Roger Garaudy, "Structuralisme et 'Mort de l'Homme'" in *La Pensée* (October 1967).
6. See Mikel Dufrenne, *Pour l'Homme* (Paris: Seuil, 1968).
7. Francis Macdonald Cornford, *The Republic of Plato* (New York and London: Oxford University Press, 1964), 507d–e, p. 218.
8. *Republic* 507d–e, pp. 218–19.
9. *Republic* 508a–b, p. 219.
10. *Republic* 510b.
11. *Republic* 504d.
12. *Republic* 509b.
13. *Symposium* 199c–212a.
14. *Republic* 490b.
15. Descartes, *Rules for the Guidance of our Mental Powers*, in *Philosophical Writings* (London: Macmillan, 1952), pp. 3–5.
16. Ibid., p. 4.
17. John Locke, *An Essay Concerning Human Understanding* (New York: Dover, 1959), vol. 1, p. 30.
18. Descartes, *Rules*, pp. 3–6.
19. Blaise Pascal, *Pensées* (Paris: Garnier, 1964), no. 253, p. 143.
20. Pascal, *Pensées*, no. 530, p. 205
21. Pensées, nos. 510 and 512, pp. 201–2; nos. 691–92, pp. 257–58.
22. *Pensées*, nos. 82 and 83, pp. 95–99; no. 282, pp. 147–48.
23. *Pensées*, no. 144, p. 115.
24. *Pensées* no. 327, p. 158.
25. Hegel, *The Phenomenology of Mind* (New York: Harper Torchbooks, 1967), Foreword, p. 99.
26. Ludwig Feuerbach, *The Essence of Christianity* (New York: Harper and Brothers, 1937), pp. 1 and 2.
27. See Noam Chomsky, *Cartesian Linguistics* (New York: Harper, 1966), pp. 3–30.
28. Feuerbach, *The Essence of Christianity*, p. 3.
29. Ibid., p. xlii.
30. Ibid., p. xliii.

136   *Notes*

31. Ibid., p. xxxviii.
32. Ibid., p. xli.
33. Ibid., pp. 4 and 5.
34. Johann Gottlieb Fichte, *Werke* (Leipzig: Eckardt, 1910), vol. 2, First Introduction to the Wissenschaftslehre, p. 6: "Merke auf dich selbst: kehre deinen Blick von allem, was dich umgibt, ab, und in dein Inneres; ist die erste Forderung, welche die Philosophie an ihren Lehrling tut. . . ."
35. Feuerbach, *The Essence of Christianity*, p. xxxvi.
36. Ibid., p. 5.
37. Max Scheler, *La idea del hombre y la historia* (Buenos Aires: Siglo XX, 1959).
38. Max Scheler, *Man's Place in Nature* (Boston: Beacon Press, 1961), pp 5 and 6.
39. Ernst Cassirer, *An Essay on Man* (New Haven: Yale University Press, 1964), Part I, chapter 1: The Crisis in Man's Knowledge of Himself.
40. Scheler, *La idea del hombre y la historia*, p. 10.
41. Cf. the title of chapter 3 of *Man's Place in Nature*, "Spirit and Life,"
42. Scheler, *Man's Place in Nature*, pp. 6 and 7.
43. Ibid., chapter 1: "The Stages of Psychophysical Life in Plant, Animal and Man," pp. 8–34.
44. Ibid., pp. 35 and 36.
45. Ibid., p. 37.
46. Ibid., p. 47.
47. Ibid., pp. 52–54.
48. Ibid., p. 47.
49. Ibid., p. 48.
50. Ibid., pp. 4 and 6.
51. Scheler, *La idea del hombre y la historia*, pp. 9 and 10.
52. Ibid., pp. 15 and 16.
53. George Lukács, *History and Class Consciousness* (Cambridge, Mass.: MIT Press, 1971), p. 10.
54. Lukács, *History and Class Consciousness*, p. 7.
55. Ibid., p. 11.
56. Ibid., p. 12.
57. Ibid., p. 14.
58. Ibid., pp. 14 and 15.
59. See Joseph Gabel's attempt, in *False Consciousness* (New York: Harper and Row, 1975), to investigate the pathology of human consciousness ("false consciousness") through a boldly promiscuous combination of Marxist-Lukacsian and psychopathological categories.
60. Lukács, *History and Class Consciousness*, chapter entitled "Reification and the Consciousness of the Proletariat," pp. 83–209.
61. "False totality" (instead of "concrete totality") is the term used by Karel Kosik in his *Dialectics of the Concrete* (Dordrecht, Holland and Boston: D. Reidel, 1967),

p. 27. Kosik implicitly appropriates Lukács's exegesis of the "fetishism of merchandise" in *Capital*, drawing epistemological and methodological conclusions from that chapter.

62. Lukács, *History and Class Consciousness*, p. 10.

63. Ibid., pp. 13–24.

64. Emile Durkheim, *The Rules of Sociological Method* (New York: The Free Press; London: Collier-Macmillan, 1964).

65. For a criticism of this point of view, see Quentin Gibson, *The Logic of Social Enquiry* (London: Routledge and Kegan Paul; New York: Humanities Press, 1960), Part I: Anti-Scientific Views About Social Enquiry.

66. Claude Lévi-Strauss, *The Savage Mind* (London: Weidenfeld and Nicolson, 1966), chapter 9: History and Dialectics.

67. Lucien Goldmann, *The Human Sciences and Philosophy* (London: Cape, 1969), esp. chapter 1.

68. Martin Heidegger, *Being and Time* (New York: Harper and Row, 1962), p. 22.

69. Ibid., pp. 71–75.

70. For example Karl Löwith's accusation that Heidegger's late work is incoherent because it breaks away from *Being and Time*. Whereas the early work is organized around an investigation of Dasein (and an analytical approach to Dasein), the later work—especially the *Letter on Humanism*—instead of directing the inquiry into Being by clarifying the structure of the questioning entity, begins directly with Being as the condition of this very questioning. One should speak of a methodological reorientation rather than a "break." See Fernando Montero's preliminary study in this regard.

In *Being and Time* Heidegger searches for the "condition of possibility" (in a clearly Kantian sense) of the question of Being. This "transcendent" element is Dasein. Heidegger later pushed his transcendental approach to the limit—its own precise limits—by inquiring about the "conditions of possibility" of Dasein. It is a surprising and rigorous investigation. To the contrary of what Löwith says, it does not suffer from a lack of rigor and coherence but rather from an excess of the same. In effect, the inquiry that he undertakes is endless. . . . It is directed "vers la découvert d'une possibilité plus reculée, d'un trascendental du trascendental: la question de la possibilité devient la question de la possibilité de la possibilité. D'où l'invocation d'instances à majuscule, dont la suprême est l'Être. Au-delà de l'homme qui nie le Néant qui neantit; au-delà de l'artiste qui crée, l'Art qui produit l'artiste et l'oeuvre; au-delà du penseur, la Pensée qui pense; au-delà du trascendental tel qu'il peut definir une subjectivité, la Trascendence qui ne designe plus seulement l'intentionalité de la conscience, mais un mouvement absolu de dépassement; au-delà de tout étant, l'Être." Dufrenne, *Pour l'Homme*, p. 18.

71. Martin Heidegger, *Letter on Humanism*, in *Basic Writings* (New York: Harper and Row, 1977), p. 236 et seq.

72. This should be clearly understood: it is a never-ending path. It never ends

because it makes the stroller walk in circles. It is the cul-de-sac that obliges us to retrace our steps in an endless process of backtracking. Whoever walks down Heidegger's path is a genuine Sisyphus who never comes to the end of his journey, i.e., to Being. Being is impermanent. When it supposedly "reveals" itself it is actually concealing itself. "Man" can only "care" for Being by freeing himself from *his own* (anthropological) structures—by somehow dehumanizing himself, denying his identity as "man" and "subject."

By this I do not mean to lend credence to the old business about the "senselessness" of Heidegger's statements. All of these lovely stories that at one time thrilled the cautious philosophers who jealously guarded their specialization and dreaded the prospect of unemployment rest on a magnificent awareness of what is normal and what is "pathological" in language. If Heidegger's language is "pathological," we might well ask "By whose standards?" If we are still told "According to the (syntactic) Norm," we must answer that we are "men of little faith," despite what we have heard from the gospel of Logic.

73. Karl Marx and Friedrich Engels, *The German Ideology* (New York: International Publishers, 1968), p. 198.

74. Ibid., p. 15.

75. Alain Robbe-Grillet, *For a New Novel* (New York: Grove Press, 1965), p. 29.

76. Alain Robbe-Grillet, *La Maison de Rendez-vous* (New York: Grove Press, 1966), p. 1.

77. Ibid., p. 9.

78. Ibid., p. 167.

Index

Adam, 26
Arnault, Antoine, 87
Althusser, Louis, 61, 74, 75; *For Marx*, 135*n*4; *Reading Capital*, 134*n*23
Amiot, M., 134*n*25
Aquinas, St. Thomas, 5
Aristotle, 20, 99
Attica, 21
Augustine, Saint, 104

Bacon, Sir Francis, 104
Balibar, Etienne: *Reading Capital*, 134*n*23
Bergson, Henri, 43
Berkeley, George, 14, 33
Boas, Franz, 74, 126

Caillois, Roger: *The Dream and Human Societies*, 134*n*31
Calvary, 49
Carnap, Rudolf, 21, 22, 23, 30, 35, 37, 43, 133*n*2; *The Logical Structure of the World*, 134*n*18
Cartesianism, 38, 43, 48, 51, 52, 55, 86, 87, 88, 89, 90, 91, 92, 93–94, 96, 101, 105, 135*n*27

Cassirer, Ernst, 5, 104; *An Essay on Man*, 136*n*39; *The Problem of Knowledge*, 133*n*2
Chomsky, Noam, 127; *Cartesian Linguistics*, 135*n*27
Christianity, 135*nn*26, 28, 29, 30; 136*nn*31, 32, 33, 35, 36
Christie, Agatha, 128
Copernican Revolution, 90–93, 94, 99–104, 109
Cornford, Francis M., 47, 134*n*19; *The Republic of Plato*, 135*n*7

Darwin, Charles, 104
Dasein, 37, 118, 119, 137*n*70
Descartes, René, 18, 31 32, 37, 42, 46, 47, 49, 56, 76, 78, 85, 87, 89, 90, 91, 99, 133*n*6; *Meditations*, 18, 46, 48; *Regulae ad Directionem Ingenii*, 46, 133*n*6, 135*nn*15, 16, 18
Dilthey, Wilhelm, 117
Dionysus, 83
Dufrenne, Mikel, 75; *Pour l'Homme*, 135*n*6, 137*n*70
Dumézil, G., 133*n*1
Durkheim, Emile, 74; *The Rules of Sociological Method*, 137*n*64